The Lover Boy of Bahawalpur

The Lover Boy of Bahawalpur

How the Pulwama Case Was Cracked

Rahul Pandita

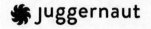

JUGGERNAUT BOOKS
C-I-128, First Floor, Sangam Vihar, Near Holi Chowk,
New Delhi 110080, India

First published by Juggernaut Books 2021

10 9 8 7 6 5 4 3 2 1

P-ISBN: 9789391165109
E-ISBN: 9789391165116

Typeset in Adobe Caslon Pro by R. Ajith Kumar, Noida

Printed at Thomson Press India Ltd

For Ma, whom I will meet again
by the Sind river in Kangan

Contents

If the red slayer think he slays,
Or if the slain think he is slain,
They know not well the subtle ways
I keep, and pass, and turn again

– 'Brahma', Ralph Waldo Emerson

1

The Man with Shaky Hands

Pulwama, South Kashmir. 14 February 2019.

The blue car wobbled slightly over the potholed road of Hajibal in Pulwama district. A few minutes later, at 3 p.m., it crossed the small bridge over the Jhelum river. The driver, Shakir Bashir, a young man in his early twenties, looked at his only co-passenger, Adil Ahmed Dar, who sat next to him. Dar, almost the same age as the driver, looked straight ahead; he was reciting something in a low tone that the driver recognized as verses from the Koran.

Shakir stopped after crossing the bridge. Then he got down and walked to the other side of the car. His friend also got down, and they exchanged seats. Dar drove the car ahead.

By 3.10 p.m., they could see the national highway in front of them that connected the Kashmir Valley to the rest of India.

Dar took a right turn and kept driving on the narrow link road that ran parallel to the highway. After driving a mile or so, they halted at a point from where they could take a U-turn and get on the highway.

Both men got down again and stood facing each other. Dar's hands were shaking, which he tried to control. He took off his electronic wristwatch that he wore at all times and gave it to his friend.

'This is something to remember me by,' he said. 'Keep me in your prayers.'

'May Allah be with you,' said Shakir. They hugged. Dar sat back in the car, leaving his friend behind. As he turned the key, he patted his jacket pocket, checking for the pistol inside. His friend waved to him; he watched the car speed up on the highway towards Srinagar.

~

In his bus, Constable H. Guru of the Central Reserve Police Force (CRPF) was reminded of his wife, Kalavathi – they had married only six months ago.

Guru's bus was part of a convoy that had started from Jammu early that morning at 3.30 a.m. Convoys carrying military personnel from Jammu to Srinagar, around 300 kilometres apart, always commenced their journey in the wee hours of the morning. This was to ensure that the stretch from Qazigund, from where the Kashmir Valley began, to Srinagar, could be covered before darkness fell, after which security forces became more vulnerable to terrorist attacks.

The CRPF convoy was bigger than usual this morning; it consisted of seventy-eight vehicles, mostly buses, carrying 2,547 personnel. It had snowed for more than a week, due to which the Jammu–Srinagar highway had been closed. So a week's worth of soldiers were being ferried in one go. The transit camps in Jammu had been overflowing with soldiers – like Guru – from all over India, headed for their duty stations in the Kashmir Valley.

After marriage, Guru had begun construction of a new house. About a fortnight ago, he had gone home to spend time with his family in Karnataka's Mandya district. He had reported back on duty three days earlier, on 11 February, but had to wait in Jammu till the highway was cleared of snow and the transport services could resume.

Earlier that day, Guru had spoken to his mother. And now he wanted to speak to his wife as well. Guru took out his mobile phone and dialled Kalavathi. The phone kept ringing, but she did not answer. She was busy with some household chore.

Guru, 33, had joined the CRPF in 2011. His first posting was in one of the Maoist-affected areas in Jharkhand in east India, and he had been transferred to Kashmir a year ago, in 2018.

In the mid-2000s, when the CRPF had taken over from the Border Security Force (BSF) as the main paramilitary force fighting Islamist militants in Kashmir, the situation was way better than in 2018. The left-wing extremist (LWE) areas in central and eastern India, on the other hand, where the CRPF fought Maoist guerrillas, had become a nightmare from the mid-2000s. The poorly trained paramilitary soldiers who had little idea about the terrain in those parts were no match for the highly motivated guerrillas who knew the area well and were experts in improvised explosive devices (IEDs), using these to target the soldiers to devastating effect. In the worst-ever attack on security forces, the Maoists in April 2010 had triggered off a blast and then engaged a CRPF party in a fierce gun battle, killing seventy-five of them.

It was the biggest casualty in any theatre of insurgency in India. The weather in these parts was humid, and the condition inside the barracks was poor. Malaria was rampant, and scores of soldiers became prey to it. Back then, a CRPF soldier would have preferred Kashmir to LWE areas. In Kashmir there were very few targeted attacks on the forces, and after years of experience, the police and the CRPF had become adept at handling stone throwers.

But around 2015 onwards, while the situation had improved significantly in LWE areas, in Kashmir it had worsened drastically. The forces were again getting targeted like they had been in the 1990s, when the insurgency was at its peak in the Valley. Terrorist attacks increased in frequency, and many soldiers lost their lives in these. The situation turned particularly volatile after security forces killed Burhan Wani, the young Kashmiri commander of the terrorist organization Hizbul Mujahideen in South Kashmir in July 2016.

At the start of the Kashmir Valley, right after the CRPF convoy crossed the Jawahar tunnel and entered Qazigund, sixteen buses were replaced with armoured vehicles. Usually, there are enough of these to carry every soldier, but this time the number of personnel in the convoy was much more than normal. The bulletproof vehicles accommodated as many soldiers as they could, and the rest continued their journey in ordinary buses.

As the convoy began to move from there, Constable Vasudev from Telangana, who was travelling in the same bus as Guru and had got off to relieve himself, hopped back in what he thought was his bus but turned out to be another one. There was hardly any space in this one, but Vasudev requested an assistant sub-inspector, R.K. Pandey, to move a little and squeezed himself next to him.

By this time, the road opening party (ROP) of the CRPF was, as usual, in place along the highway. As convoys move from one place to another in Kashmir, the ROP keeps a check on attempts to plant explosives underneath roads to blow up vehicles. It also stops the lateral movement of vehicles from smaller roads into the path of the convoy till it crosses that particular stretch. The movement of vehicles already on the highway was allowed.

Meanwhile, inside Guru's bus, bearing the registration number HR49F-0637, number five in the convoy, Head Constable Sukhjinder Singh, 32, recorded a video on his mobile phone and WhatsApped it to his wife, Sarabjit Kaur, in Tarn Taran, Punjab. Singh had joined the force in 2003 and was to retire in 2022; he planned to settle in Canada afterwards.

Singh had made a call to his family that morning.

Speaking to his elder brother, Singh inquired about his health and said he would call again that evening. He had become a father a year ago and had taken off in January for his son's first Lohri, a festival celebrated widely in Punjab. As Sukhjinder left his village to join duty back in the Valley, he, like Guru and many others, had to wait in Jammu's transit camp before he could be moved to his duty post in Kashmir.

Singh was on one of the front seats. In the video he sent to his wife, the mobile camera turns left, showing a soldier dozing off on another seat. Then it veers back in front of Singh's seat where some bags are kept. Then he flips the camera towards himself, revealing a hardened but handsome face. Outside, mounds of dirty snow on the side of the road are visible.

The bus was driven by Head Constable Jaimal Singh, 44, who came from Moga district neighbouring Tarn Taran. He too was returning from leave to visit his family, particularly to see his six-year-old son, who was born sixteen years after his marriage. The designated driver of the bus was someone else, but he had proceeded on leave for his son's wedding. Jaimal Singh had been asked to fill in for him.

In the same bus, another constable from Uttar Pradesh, Pradeep Kumar, was on the phone with his wife, Neerja. He was also joining duty after a brief leave and had reached Jammu on 11 February.

At 3.15 p.m., the convoy was speeding along on the four-lane highway in Pulwama in South Kashmir, less than a thirty-minute drive from Srinagar.

In another bus, a little behind in the convoy, Constable Jaswinder saw the blue car with Dar behind the wheel overtaking them. Less than a 100 metres from where they were there is a steep rise in gradient and a bend on the road because of which heavy vehicles slow down a bit. There are no houses on the right at this spot, only a hillock with a few communication towers and a wall in front, advertising 'Pepsi' and 'Swift Homes Modular Kitchens'. There are a few houses on the left, a little below the elevated highway. Behind these houses, the Jhelum makes its way towards Srinagar and then onward to North Kashmir, flowing soon afterwards into Pakistan-occupied Kashmir.

At that point on the highway, as part of the ROP, Assistant Sub-Inspector Mohan Lal saw the blue car swerve and get between two buses. Something was not right. He cocked his rifle and began running towards the car.

In CCTV camera footage of that moment, a few buses of the CRPF convoy – five or six – are seen, with another civilian car, a red one, following right behind. It must have overtaken other buses in the convoy, and, as the car begins to overtake one more, a flash is seen erupting a little ahead of it.

A few seconds earlier Constable Pradeep Kumar, sitting in the bus, had asked his wife about their younger daughter, Manya, and before she could answer, the phone got disconnected. She tried calling back, but she found her husband's phone was switched off.

The blue car had rammed into the bus, carrying Guru, Sukhjinder, Jaimal, Pradeep and thirty-five others. Two hundred kg of explosives kept in the rear of the car exploded as the man with shaky hands pressed a small switch beneath the car's steering wheel.

The blast could be heard miles away. In one of the houses below the road, a few children were playing in their garden. A moment after the deafening explosion a bloodied torso landed amidst them. Pieces of human flesh, shards of glass and shrapnel flew all over. The bus was completely destroyed, killing all thirty-nine soldiers, and Mohan Lal of the ROP. His friend, standing on duty just 200 metres away, rushed towards him, but Lal had been blown to pieces by the impact of the blast.

Inside their buses, the CRPF soldiers were left stunned. In some buses, the personnel kept sitting for more than ten minutes, too shocked to act. They could hear gunfire but were not sure if it came from terrorists or from some of their own.

A rescue team of the Indian Army that rushed from their nearby Pampore base was the first to reach the spot a few minutes later. It found the mangled remains of four soldiers dangling over the communication towers, on the other side of the road.

It was the deadliest terrorist attack in Kashmir in its three bloody decades of insurgency. Kashmir was no stranger to violence. But such a brazen attack – perhaps the most brazen since the one in October 2001 on the state legislative assembly that killed twenty-four civilians and eleven security personnel – had been carried out after a long time in the Valley.

When Vasudev – whose life was saved when he inadvertently got on to the wrong bus at Qazigund – stepped out of his bus, the first man he called was Suneem Khan, a Kashmiri doctor working with the CRPF. Khan had just entered the auditorium in the nearby army cantonment to watch the film *Gully Boy* when his phone rang.

'*Sir, sab khatam ho gaya.*' Everything is finished, the distraught Vasudev said from the other side.

Khan ran out, shouting for his driver. In seventeen

minutes, he was at the scene of the attack. What Khan witnessed there, he described later to a friend, was an apocalypse. Body parts were strewn all over. There was a head here, a finger there, a piece of an intestine. And blood.

'It was as if there was a curtain of blood, stretching till the horizon,' recalled a CRPF officer who reached the site shortly after the attack. A senior CRPF officer wept inconsolably at the sight, and for twenty-four hours he could not put down his pack of cigarettes.

2

A Key Numbered 1026

The next morning, on 15 February, Rakesh Balwal stood at the spot of the suicide attack, looking at the metal scrap the targeted bus had been reduced to. All around him teams of forensic and explosive experts scoured the area, looking for evidence. Balwal, an officer from the Manipur cadre of the Indian Police Service, had taken over as the Jammu and Kashmir (J&K) head of the National Investigation Agency (NIA) in July 2018.

The NIA was created in 2009 on the lines of America's Federal Bureau of Investigation (FBI) to carry out investigations that would hold up under international scrutiny. It came into being through an act of Parliament in the aftermath of the 2008 Mumbai terror attack.

A police officer associated with the agency at its inception reminisced how sometimes at international forums, dossiers on terrorists or terrorist organizations submitted by India would be dismissed because of shoddy evidence. 'The investigation we put forth on cross-border terrorism would be mocked at,' he recalled. 'They would say our dossiers looked like Wikipedia entries.' The NIA was known to take the best from among India's police forces to work on important cases such as the Pulwama attack and provide foolproof evidence for prosecution.

In October 2017, as the police chief of Manipur's Churachandpur district, Balwal had been instrumental in busting an international human trafficking racket, resulting in the rescue of fourteen girls from Myanmar. His experience in dealing with the complex web of insurgencies in the Northeast had made his superiors at the NIA offer him a position in the organization. He also belonged to the Jammu region and knew the state well.

In his late thirties, Balwal liked his hair short. He kept fit by running, and despite the gruelling schedule of his job, took out time to go on hikes with his family. Among journalists in the state, he had a reputation for being non-approachable. In Kashmir, soon they would know him as the man from Jammu who went doggedly after the perpetrators of the Pulwama attack. Standing on the highway in Pulwama that morning, Balwal felt a sense of gloom. It was an extremely cold day, and though Balwal wore an overcoat, draughts of chilly air needled through his clothing, making him shiver. One side of the highway had been opened for traffic, and the shops around the site had opened as well. But as investigation teams searched the area, every now and then someone would come back with a finger or a part of a bone or a piece of skin. It was a difficult thing to watch, so much so that the inspector general of police in Kashmir, S.P. Pani, a seasoned police officer, could not control his emotions at the site and his eyes turned moist.

The suicide attack had shaken the security grid in Kashmir. Many officers feared that other similar attacks may take place. 'Let me say everyone was a little nervous, especially of vehicles coming close to theirs as they moved around on duty,' recalled a senior police officer.

Balwal tried to speak to other CRPF men in the convoy, but most of them were in extreme shock. They all knew each other, and, as they began to remember their dead colleagues, many of them cried. The trauma was so severe that even those who were just behind the targeted bus could not remember anything.

Less than fifteen minutes after the blast, a video of the suicide bomber had been released by the Pakistan-based terrorist organization Jaish-e-Mohammed. The young man, it came to be known, was Adil Ahmed Dar, a resident of Kakapora, Pulwama, not far from the blast site.

In the video, Dar is seen holding an M4 carbine gun in one hand and a Browning pistol in the other. There are guns and grenades arranged around him, and behind him there is a Jaish flag. 'Don't get swayed by Western influences with which the enemy wants to sidetrack you from the glorious path of Islam,' he tells young Kashmiris. Dar calls India a nation of cow-piss drinkers, saying a destruction it cannot deal with will come its way. 'In the past as well we have inflicted scars on your being,' he continued, mentioning the IC-814 hijacking and the Parliament attack, among other terrorist attacks.

As investigators closely examined the video, they found a peculiar thing: Dar's lip movement had been made to sync with somebody else's voice. The investigators found it perplexing. Why would the Jaish need to do this?

In the meantime, as journalists rushed to Dar's house and spoke to his father, Ghulam Hassan Dar, a story much like hundreds of others from Kashmir came to the fore. Dar had dropped out of class twelve and started working in a sawmill. A little later, in March

2018, his picture had appeared on social media in the usual format that terrorist organizations in Kashmir follow when they have to announce a new recruit: Dar holds a gun in the backdrop of a Jaish flag; his nom de guerre is Waqas Commando.

Just another day in Kashmir, just another young man gone astray. Just another day for the police as well, who included Dar's name in the list of terrorists active in the area. They knew that like his peers, it was just a matter of weeks before he would be holed up in some building and get killed.

But nobody had imagined the destruction he would wreak.

As journalists talked to Dar's father, he offered up a familiar story that every father of a terrorist repeats in Kashmir. He said Dar had felt humiliated after policemen beat him up a few years ago; he said he had no idea his son had turned into a suicide bomber. It would later become clear that Dar's father knew his son had embarked on a dangerous path.

As Dar's video statement went viral over social media, a Jaish spokesperson also contacted a local news organization in Kashmir, claiming responsibility for the attack. Immediately afterwards, the mobile phone used to make that call was traced by investigators to

Rawalpindi in Pakistan but it was found to be switched off. The SIM card used to make the call was in the name of a Kashmiri woman who had already passed away.

Before the CRPF could even officially provide the exact figure of the dead to the NIA, the Jaish released it in their magazine, *Al-Qalam*, leaving many surprised.

The suicide attack had created confusion in the security establishment in Kashmir. Many believed that it was carried out by a Pakistani terrorist and that Dar's name was used to falsely portray to the international community that the insurgency in Kashmir was indigenous and that 'India's occupation' in Kashmir was forcing ordinary Kashmiris to turn into suicide bombers. Some believed that Adil Dar had recorded his video for some other attack and had later been killed, and now the Jaish was mischievously propping him up as the bomber.

'I met a senior intelligence officer who believed in this theory,' recalled an investigator. 'He told me that Kashmiris did not have the guts to blow themselves up.'

If some in the security grid were sceptical about a Kashmiri being a suicide bomber, there was reason behind it. There had been only one Kashmiri suicide bomber till then – a seventeen-year-old medical student, Afaq Ahmed Shah, who blew himself up in an explosive-laden car at the main gate of the Army's 15 Corps headquarters in Srinagar in April 2000, killing two soldiers. Another young woman had died in a blast in 2006 in South Kashmir, but she was just a courier and the bomb she was carrying accidentally exploded on her person, blowing her to pieces.

It was generally true that as compared to foreign terrorists who were well trained in camps in Pakistan and Afghanistan, the Kashmiri militants did not have the same zeal and training. The foreigners, mostly Pakistanis, like the Mumbai terror attacker Ajmal Kasab, came from poor families and were filled with hatred in madrasas. They would hold in their minds an image of Kashmir that was far removed from reality. The stories they were told portrayed that the Muslim majority in Kashmir was getting brutalized by the Hindu majoritarian state of India. These would be as grim as how Muslims were not allowed to offer prayers in mosques and how the Hindus had occupied all the mosques. Motivated to take revenge to 'save' Islam, the jihadis would then be pushed across the border, in many cases to launch what came to be known as fidayeen attacks.

From a border town along the Line of Control (LoC) in Kashmir, a Kashmiri sympathizer would give them shelter and then drive them to the target to launch the attack. Once out on the streets, sometimes these men would realize the fallacy of what they had been told. But by this time there would be no turning back.

They would open fire and enter a building and hold on for as long as they could. The security forces would surround it, and the encounter would last a few hours or a few days. But barring a few exceptions, it always ended in the death of the terrorists; many times security forces would also lose their lives. But certainly nothing close to the number of dead in the Pulwama attack.

In 2008, the J&K Police arrested one such foreign terrorist before he could carry out an attack. Upon receiving a tip-off from the Intelligence Bureau (IB), a police team raided a hotel in Delhi's Paharganj area and arrested the man. After sustained interrogation, the man revealed that he had been trained in Pakistan and Saudi Arabia and had been flown from Rawalpindi, Pakistan, to Dhaka, Bangladesh, from where he crossed into West Bengal, finally reaching Kolkata. The money for his launch, he said, was provided by a Pakistani national based in Singapore.

In Kolkata he realized the stories he had been told in Pakistan were all lies. 'Everywhere I went, even in visibly Hindu-dominated areas, I could hear the azaan rising from mosques all over,' he would later tell his interrogators.

When he was arrested in Delhi he had been inviting prostitutes to his room, arranged by a Hindu pimp.

~

On 16 February, teams of the Central Forensic Science Laboratory (CFSL), the NIA's bomb experts, and a team from the National Bomb Data Centre of the National Security Guard (NSG) visited the spot in Pulwama and picked up samples. Separate boxes were kept for body pieces, metal and residue of explosives.

'We were putting together whatever we could of bodies. We placed them in caskets but explained to family members how it would be. They understood,' an officer involved in the preliminary investigation said.

A senior CRPF officer in one of the districts in Uttar Pradesh who was to receive one of the bodies rang up a colleague in Kashmir.

'Poora hai ya aadha?' Is it whole or half? he asked, referring to the remains of the fallen soldier.

'Do not open the box,' his friend from Kashmir replied.

Parts of the engine and chassis of the car used in the

attack were found, but it yielded no information. Its markings had been erased carefully. A dead end.

On 18 February, a team from Maruti arrived in Kashmir and examined the car's crankshaft found at the blast site. They opened it up to reveal a batch number in its innards. From this number, the Maruti experts traced it to an Eeco car model that was rolled out of the factory on 25 January 2011. The records at Maruti showed that on that day seven Eeco cars were manufactured; only one of them made its way to Kashmir. The vehicle used in the attack had chassis number MA3ERLF1SOO183735 and engine number G12BN164140. On further investigation they realized that the car had been sent to a prominent Maruti car dealer in Kashmir, Peaks Auto Private Limited.

The same day the owner of the car, one Jaleel Ahmed Haqqani, was picked up; he had bought the car soon after it had landed in the showroom in Kashmir. He told the police that he had sold off the car later. As the police began tracing the car further, they learnt that it had been sold six more times since then. The investigators could not afford to lose time; one by one the subsequent owners of the car were picked up in order to reach the person who had last bought the car. Those who were picked up were kept in detention so that the leads in the investigation remained a secret.

As the chain moved forward, the investigators got hold of a man named Danish Ahmed Lone. One of the owners had informed them that Lone had acted as an agent in the sale to the next man. As Lone was interrogated, he told the investigators that the man he had sold the car to happened to be his cousin, Sajjad Bhat. He also revealed the car had been sold to Bhat towards the end of January 2019 for Rs 1.85 lakh and that he had made a profit of Rs 15,000 by way of commission.

As the NIA went looking for Bhat, they found that he hadn't been home for a number of days. 'It looked like he had realized we were zeroing in upon him,' said an investigator. The trail stopped right there.

Six days passed. There were murmurs that the attack was a big intelligence failure and that nobody had a clue how so much explosive (RDX, many reports said) could have made its way into the Kashmir Valley without getting detected.

The politics over the attack had also begun immediately. The critics of India's Prime Minister Narendra Modi felt that the attack had dented his steely image and had also exposed what they called the incompetence of India's national security adviser, Ajit Doval. In the crazy echo chambers of social media, many suggested that the attack could have been the handiwork of the government as it wanted to deflect attention from its failings and had thus orchestrated the attack to trigger a wave of patriotic sentiment before the Lok Sabha elections two months later.

The politics over questions of nationalism and patriotism had sharpened since one particular night in 2016 in Delhi's Jawaharlal Nehru University (JNU) during an event to commemorate the death anniversary of Afzal Guru, a Kashmiri Jaish operative, hanged to death three years earlier for his role in the 2001 Parliament attack. That evening, as students looked on, a few people, some of them wearing masks, appeared at the event and shouted slogans which riled up many present there. Some of them hailed Guru as a martyr and said that his blood would bring about a revolution. Two slogans in particular, uttered by men with clear Kashmiri accents, had dangerous undertones: *'Bharat tere tukde honge, Inshallah, Inshallah'* (India, you will be torn into pieces, Allah willing, Allah willing); *'Bharat ki barbaadi tak jung chalegi'* (The war will continue till India's destruction).

The video clips of the event shot on mobile phones became viral, creating a nationwide furore. Many felt that the Islamist jihad in Kashmir, that had left scars several times in cities like Delhi and Mumbai, was now being normalized.

Prime Minister Modi and the Bharatiya Janata Party (BJP) had successfully managed to make the JNU incident and 'anti-nationalism' a political and electoral issue. Now, with two months to go for the 2019 general elections, the Pulwama attack had sent patriotic sentiment soaring again. This was not the first time that young soldiers from the Indian heartland had been killed in the line of duty in Kashmir. But this time, in towns and cities across India, a massive surge of sentiment took over. People got together spontaneously and came out in processions in honour of the fallen in Pulwama.

In Samastipur in Bihar, an angry procession raised anti-Pakistan slogans. Many people got emotional, including a policeman who hurled abuses at Pakistan outside the collector's office. Many in the crowd hailed Prime Minister Modi and beseeched him to take revenge.

Far away from this spectacle, played over and over again on prime-time television, the NIA team worked quietly. Bhat had gone missing and no other clue that could take the case forward was coming Balwal's way. After much deliberation he told his superiors at the NIA headquarters in Delhi that he needed to expand the area of search around the site of the attack.

But this was risky. Around the site of the suicide attack, areas like Hajibal were hotbeds of militancy. Often, as a gun battle raged on between security forces and terrorists holed up in a building, the residents in such areas would come out after being prompted by WhatsApp voice messages and attack forces with stones to help the cornered terrorists escape. In many cases, they were able to do so as security forces held their fire to avoid civilian casualties.

The J&K Police advised Balwal against it. But he felt this was the only way forward. Every other avenue had led to an impasse. And so he persisted.

Finally, on the afternoon of 20 February, after permission came through from New Delhi, a large group comprising 100 NIA and 400 CRPF personnel descended upon the area, conducting an extended search. As they spread through the area, Balwal walked towards the Jhelum river, his eyes on the ground one moment and then around him the next, in anticipation of hostile crowds. By this time, he had walked 250 metres from the site of the blast. Across the Jhelum, he could see a crowd of onlookers forming in Hajibal.

'Sir, let us speed up things here; the area is very dangerous,' a policeman cautioned him.

As Balwal walked ahead, suddenly his eye caught

something shining on the ground. When he came closer he realized the shiny object was half buried in mud slush that had frozen in the Kashmir cold. He bent down and pulled it out. It turned out to be a key with the number '1026' engraved on it. A little ahead, Balwal found a piece of bone.

The key turned out to be that of the Eeco car. A DNA profiling report on the tissue material around the bone found it to be a match with the DNA extracted from Ghulam Hassan Dar's blood sample.

It was confirmed now beyond doubt that the bomber was indeed the Kashmiri Adil Ahmed Dar.

3

The Burly Man in Bahawalpur

'Gore aaye hain.' The white people are here.

A young overground worker (OGW) of the Jaish had been assigned to keep an eye on Dar's house. OGWs like him helped terrorist organizations by providing them shelter or ferrying them from one point to another or keeping an eye on troop movement. Many of them subsequently become active militants.

On 21 February, some foreign journalists came visiting at Dar's house. The OGW took out his phone and recorded a voice message. And then he tapped on the screen to send it.

The message didn't have to go far. Had the man walked a bit, a few miles, he could have delivered it personally to his boss, 'the commander', a man wearing a Sindhi ajrak cap.

Inside the house a couple of miles away, the commander was chatting with a young woman. He was living with her family and had told her that he loved her. His mobile beeped. *'Gore aaye hain.'*

The commander got very excited at the message from the OGW. He recorded a voice note and sent it off. In the message to his uncle, a burly man sitting in Bahawalpur in Pakistan, who was also his boss, he said this was a great opportunity to target foreigners and create a sensation by bumping them off.

He didn't have to wait long for his boss's reply.

'Picchle kaam ka lutf uthao. Thoda itminaan rakho,' he heard his uncle's voice. The burly man in Bahawalpur asked his nephew to enjoy the fruits of his previous work and to be patient. Nothing was to be done right now.

~

On 23 February, the NIA raided Sajjad Bhat's house. In their investigation, they found that Bhat, like the suicide bomber Adil Dar, had studied till class twelve and then joined the Siraj-ul-Uloom, a religious seminary associated with the Jamaat-e-Islami, Jammu and Kashmir (JIJK), in the neighbouring Shopian district. His father also happened to be a Jamaati, as the organization's followers are called. The Jamaat in J&K was seen as the fountainhead of Islamist secessionist movement in the Valley. The terrorist organization Hizbul Mujahideen, fighting for Kashmir's merger with Pakistan, has its roots in the JIJK. On 28 February 2019, the Centre declared the Jamaat-e-Islami in J&K an 'unlawful organization' and said that it 'is in close touch with militant outfits and is supporting extremism and militancy in J&K and elsewhere'.

But before that, on 25 February, Bhat's photo appeared on social media, brandishing an AK-47 rifle to announce that he had officially joined the Jaish in one of its fidayeen squads and had been given the code name of Afzal Guru. The Jaish would make it a point to invoke Guru's name again and again to attract Kashmiri youth into its fold.

The burly man in Bahawalpur frowned as he looked at the picture of Bhat holding the AK-47 rifle, which he had received on his cell phone from the Jaish commander wearing the Sindhi ajrak cap.

'Ask him to sit straight lest General Bakshi* tells the world again that our martyrs are high on drugs,' he

---

* G.D. Bakshi, a retired Indian Army general who often appeared in TV discussions with an aggression that became his hallmark.

spoke gravely into his mobile phone. And then he sent the recorded message to the commander.

'May Allah be with you,' the burly man signed off.

~

'They are congratulating him.'

According to intelligence sources, the young man whom everyone was congratulating, Mudasir Khan, was from Pulwama, too. He had been under the police's scanner since the beginning of 2018 in connection with two attacks on security forces, one in Jammu and the other in Kashmir.

On 10 February 2018, at about 5 a.m., four heavily armed terrorists wearing army fatigues attacked the Sunjuwan army camp on the outskirts of Jammu city, barely a few miles from its university. Five soldiers and the father of a soldier were killed in the attack; the pregnant wife of a soldier also got shot in the back. The attackers were later neutralized.

In their investigation, the police found out that the recce of the camp for the attack was done by a Jaish OGW identified as Mudasir Khan, a resident of Tral area in Pulwama. This was the man, intelligence sources said, that people were congratulating after the Pulwama attack.

A few weeks before the Jammu attack, the Jaish had carried out another attack, on a CRPF camp in Pulwama, close to where the suicide attack took place in 2019. The attack on the CRPF camp was carried out on 31 December 2017, at about 2 a.m., by three terrorists who threw grenades and opened fire at the guards. Four CRPF personnel were killed in the attack, while an officer trapped inside a building died due to a heart attack.

An encounter followed that lasted for ten hours. Ultimately, the three terrorists, including the sixteen-year-old son of a policeman who had joined the Jaish a few months earlier, were killed by security forces. The sixteen-year-old and one of his two accomplices were from Pulwama itself, while the third terrorist was from Rawalkot in Pakistan-occupied Kashmir.

Mudasir Khan, the police learnt, was involved in planning this attack as well. He had disappeared in January 2018, right after the attack on the CRPF camp, and had been on the run since then.

As Mudasir's name surfaced again, the NIA began to look for him with fresh vigour. Investigators learned from an informant that he had been operating his WhatsApp through a virtual private network (VPN). A VPN allows a user to establish a private connection to the internet, masking the user's internet protocol (IP) address with one provided by the VPN, making the user anonymous. Terrorists and their sympathizers use this to avoid getting tracked down by security agencies. A few days after the Pulwama suicide attack, Mudasir, they found out, had put up a WhatsApp status: 'Who wants to be the next martyr?'

Another Jaish OGW, Bilal Ahmed Mir, had even responded to his status saying he wanted to be the next martyr. Bilal, it turned out from the messages tapped into by security agencies, was curious about who had carried out the Pulwama attack. In response to his question about it, Mudasir had sent Bilal a picture of the gelatine sticks used in making explosives.

Later, the explosive examination report would confirm that three kinds of explosives – RDX, nitroglycerine (extracted from gelatine sticks) and ammonium nitrate – were used in the blast. The investigators were sceptical because prior to this they had not seen these explosives being used together. But the forensics were certain. They said they had tested the explosives several times and had come to the same conclusion every time.

On 26 February, the NIA raided Mudasir's house. 'Convey to him the message that his days are numbered and if he does not surrender, he will soon be killed in an encounter,' an NIA officer told Mudasir's father. As they kept questioning him, Mudasir's brother, a special needs boy, was hovering around them, oblivious to what they were there for.

Mudasir's father told the NIA officials that Mudasir had a fascination for uniforms and wanted to join the police. But he could offer no explanation as to why his son had chosen to go the other way. During questioning, the father reluctantly accepted that people had been congratulating him for his son's actions.

But Mudasir Khan and Sajjad Bhat were just the foot soldiers of the attack. The real masterminds were the burly man of Bahawalpur and the Jaish commander in the ajrak cap. But the NIA didn't know this yet.

4
Balakot

Four days after the Pulwama attack, a man rode on a two-wheeler to a hilltop in Balakot in Pakistan's Khyber Pakhtunkhwa region. In the upper pocket of his shirt he had a mobile phone that beamed a live video of the area to a facility in New Delhi. The man was doing so on behalf of a handler from India's foreign intelligence agency, the Research and Analysis Wing (RAW).

The government had made clear to the security top brass on the evening of the Pulwama attack itself that it wanted to retaliate. The RAW had been asked to identify targets inside Pakistani territory that could be attacked. In response, the agency came up with three potential targets. One of them was a terrorist training camp just across the LoC in J&K.

The government rejected this option immediately.

'The government did not want this to be another Uri surgical strike,' said a senior official in the know of the operation, referring to the 2016 operation by

India's Special Forces on terror launchpads across the LoC. The other target was also rejected since it was close to a civilian facility and there were chances of collateral damage.

The third target seemed most viable. It was a Jaish training camp on a hilltop in a place called Balakot, away from civilian areas. When the RAW asset in Pakistan who would help to get images and exact coordinates of the camp was consulted, he told the RAW a vignette from Balakot's history. It is here in 1831 that the Sikh ruler Maharaja Ranjit Singh's troops killed Syed Ahmed Barelvi, a man whose dreams of establishing an Islamic caliphate preceded those of Islamist organizations such as the Islamic State of Iraq and Syria (ISIS) and who was 'the first person to realize the necessity of a movement which was at the same time religious, military and political'.* Barelvi lies buried in Balakot, a fact not lost on organizations like the Jaish that chose the place to set up training camps. Balakot as an option for a strike was both strategically viable and symbolically apt, and so the government gave the go-ahead to bomb this target.

Around the same time, a few other potential targets

---

* Olivier Roy, *Islam and Resistance in Afghanistan*, Cambridge University Press, 1986, 1990.

in Pakistan were searched on Google from various locations in India. The intelligence agencies of both countries keep an eye on locations in their country that are searched on Google in the other country. 'Let us say that if we found Parliament searched several times in Pakistan, it would send alarm bells ringing here,' said a senior Indian official. The RAW was deliberately searching for several Pakistani locations so as to keep the Pakistani agencies confused about where India could hit.

In Pakistan, Indian intelligence assets reported how the fugitive Dawood Ibrahim was getting jittery in Karachi as he thought he may be targeted by India. 'He was begging Pakistanis to shift him to Islamabad. But the Pakistanis refused as it would be difficult to explain his presence there. Instead, they shifted him to a secure bunker in Karachi itself,' said a source.

The option of killing Dawood Ibrahim was also put in front of the government. But the consensus, said the source, was that Dawood was a spent force and his killing would hardly send any message.

In the meantime, Indian surveillance reported that Pakistan was fortifying one of its brigade headquarters near the LoC across the Uri sector. 'It was so crazy that some of us joked that Pakistan has brought all its steel to fortify the complex against a potential Indian attack,' quipped an official.

Finally, as planned, the aerial strike took place in the early hours of 26 February. The munitions dropped by Mirage 2000 fighter jets hit the Jaish's training centre, destroying big parts of the complex. But it could not be ascertained how many casualties had taken place. The RAW assets reported that the several injured persons were taken to different hospitals so that the total number did not get leaked. 'We know that many of the injured who could have been saved died because they were not taken to the hospital,' revealed a source.

A day after the Balakot strike, on 27 February, Pakistani jets scrambled into Indian airspace. As Indian jets went after them, one of India's MIG-21s was hit, and the pilot, Abhinandan Varthaman, who ejected from the hit aircraft, landed in Pakistani territory and was captured by Pakistani forces.

Fearing escalation, the Pakistani authorities decided to return the pilot to India. After spending a few tense days in captivity, Varthaman returned to India on 1 March.

That day the burly man in Bahawalpur received a message from the Sindhi ajrak cap–wearing commander in Pulwama.

'*Asalam waleykum,*' wrote the commander.

'*Jeete raho,*' replied the burly man.

'Why did you let go of the Indian pilot?'

'This is all politics, my dear. Do not worry too much about it.'

'We want the war to happen. Once the border opens, all of our fighters can easily step in and defeat the infidels.'

'Yes, yes. Listen, we need to hit them once more. Get it organized in a few weeks.'

'Okay, no problem. Listen, that money still hasn't reached me.'

'It is proving to be a little difficult.'

'I have spent Rs 5.7 lakh on the attack. That money I need to return.'

'I understand. It will reach you soon; I will get it expedited.'

~

The NIA officer's warning to Mudasir's father came true quite soon. There was no clarity over how many terrorists had died in the Balakot air strike, but in Kashmir, the police and the army were asked by the Union home ministry to go after terrorists, especially those associated with the Jaish, like never before. On 10 March, Mudasir and two Pakistani terrorists were trapped in a house in Tral and killed. From 14 February till 10 March, the police claimed to have killed eighteen terrorists, fourteen of them from the Jaish. Six out of these, the police said, were of commander level in the Jaish's hierarchy.

A day after his badly burnt corpse was buried, mourners gathered at Mudasir's house, decorated with Jaish and Hizbul flags and pictures of 'martyrs' like Mudasir. The same old stories, of young men joining terrorist organizations because of police atrocities, were retold and republished.

Mudasir's father said he was expecting a last call from his son after he received news that Mudasir had been trapped.

But the call never came.

The father told the NIA that soon after the raid on their house, Mudasir had met him in an orchard and told him that his days were numbered as the police was now hunting for him. He told his father that there was no way for him to escape. 'He told me that once one enters the Jaish, there is no way to get out,' his father said.

They said of Mudasir Khan that he was a great cricketer. When he played in local matches, people would stop their work for the joy of watching him play. And now he was gone.

Shortly after Mudasir was killed the burly man in Bahawalpur received a message on his mobile from the Sindhi ajrak topi–wearing Jaish commander.

'The Indian media now thinks that Mudasir was the mastermind,' the commander said. 'They are making a fool out of their people.'

The burly man chuckled.

'*Unko gumraah rakho* (keep them astray),' the burly man replied. 'May Allah be with you,' he signed off.

~

The attack the burly man had told the Sindhi topi wearing–commander to organize a few weeks after the Pulwama strike had to be held off.

'Listen, we need to cancel the hit. There is too much pressure,' the burly man of Bahawalpur said.

'But why? We are all ready.'

'There is too much international spotlight on us.'

'*Accha.*' Okay.

'This thing has ended up helping Modi instead of damaging him. Now the fauj is after our people. Too many soldiers have died.' *'Nuksaan utna hi hona chahiye jitna dushman ko bardasht karne ki taaqat ho,'* the burly man said. The loss should be only as much as the enemy can absorb. *'Agli karwahi ki ijazat bilkul nahin hai abhi,'* he signed off. There is absolutely no permission for the next action.

5

'The Army of Mohammed' in South Kashmir

We will break here for a moment from the main story. It is important to delve into the past to understand the ground where young Kashmiris like Adil Dar, Sajjad Bhat and Mudasir Khan get radicalized, becoming fodder in a complex war in which there are no clear winners.

In the next three chapters we will find a brief history of the insurgency, understand how counterterrorism works on the ground and encounter some of the most wanted terrorists in India – Masood Azhar and his chosen lieutenants. The Pulwama attack can, in fact, be traced to the house of terror set up by Masood Azhar himself.

The insurgency had begun in the Kashmir Valley in the second half of 1988. A handful of Kashmiri men returned that summer after receiving training in arms in Pakistan-occupied Kashmir.

Severing Kashmir, the only Muslim-majority state

in India, had been a Pakistani wet dream since Partition. In October 1947, Pakistan had sent tribesmen (called Kabailis) from its Northwest Frontier Province along with army regulars to annex Kashmir, which was then still a princely state.

The raiders reached the North Kashmir town of Baramulla, killing Hindus and Sikhs, turning a cinema hall into a rape house. Kashmir's Hindu ruler, Hari Singh, sought India's help, which was granted immediately. The Indian Army landed in Kashmir and repulsed the attack, leading to the first war between India and Pakistan. Some parts of the state were gone, occupied by Pakistan, but the rest of it was saved by the Indian Army, and thus J&K became a part of India. The line till which the Pakistanis had occupied territory became the LoC – a de facto border but not the officially recognized international border, with both sides laying claims to territory occupied by the other.

In 1965, Pakistan tried again, by sending its army, masquerading as mercenary guerrillas. But the Indian authorities were alerted by a Gujjar herdsman who spotted a group of armed men near a meadow in North Kashmir where he had gone to graze his cattle. Mohammed Din Jagir, a resident of Tangmarg, was asked by these men to help them get into the town; they wanted him to arrange Kashmiri clothing for them so that they could enter without arousing suspicion. But instead of doing that, Jagir informed the police.

The information turned out to be crucial; the armed men had infiltrated the state from Pakistan to launch Operation Gibraltar, a secret Pakistani mission to annex Kashmir. It ended up in failure, thanks in part to Kashmiris like Jagir who reported such activities to the authorities, enabling India to foil Pakistan's designs.

The Centre announced a Padma Shri award for Jagir and the then prime minister, Indira Gandhi, is believed to have personally asked him if she could do something for him. Jagir asked for two things: a Philips transistor and intervention with the father of a woman he wanted to marry but who had turned him down. The transistor was gifted to him on the day he received his Padma Shri along with the likes of the scientist Satish Dhawan and the artist M.F. Husain. Later, a junior administrative officer was sent to his village. He convinced the woman's father to get his daughter married to Jagir.

In 1965, only a handful of people in Kashmir may have thought of Jagir as a traitor; nobody harmed him or burnt down his house. But in 1990, as the Islamist insurgency broke out, Jagir was killed by terrorists for his pro-India stance of twenty-five years ago. By this time, being seen as India's man in Kashmir was an unpardonable crime in the eyes of those who had picked up guns for *azaadi*.

In 1988, as the Kashmiri men who had crossed over to Pakistan for arms training returned home, they began carrying out their activities. Two bombs went off on 31 July 1988, one outside the Central Telegraph Office and one outside the Golf Course in the heart of Srinagar city. In the meantime, intelligence agencies were sending reports to the Centre about the movement along the LoC – of men crossing and of weapons being smuggled in, some of them after being tied to the belly of the sheep owned by the cattle herders in the area. The movement was made possible by Gujjar herdsmen like Jagir who knew the treacherous passes well.

Before 1990, the LoC was more or less a vague concept. The Gujjar herdsmen would often cross it from both sides, taking their cattle to meadows up there during summers. When the terrorist movement began, these men helped militants in crossing the line, over 700 kilometres long, through several routes, especially the ones falling in North Kashmir from Gurez to Keran. By the mid-2000s, the army had finally managed to erect a fence over almost half of it, but it was breached by militants and their handlers who were trained by the Pakistani Army and given special tools like wire cutters and mine detectors.

In 2009, the police in Kashmir caught hold of a man who they found out had crossed the LoC more than seventy times since 1990, bringing along terrorists and their ammunition. In his mid-fifties, the man was called Chacha (uncle) by the officer who interrogated him but was otherwise known as Gilgit Baba. The man agreed to cooperate with the police as long as his real identity was not revealed. He feared that the Pakistani agencies would harm his family that lived in Pakistan-occupied territory.

He told the interrogators that he knew the LoC well and could always fool the Indian Army as he knew their patterns, including the time when they usually patrolled. He then gave his interrogators a specific route which he claimed to have used several times. It ran close to a forward post manned by the army. The army refused to believe it, but the man was insistent. He gave proof – there was a particular spot where he said he had buried the plastic wrapper of a pack of biscuits. When that spot was searched, the wrapper was recovered, just like Gilgit Baba had claimed.

But back in 1989, even as the intelligence agencies were sending inputs about the ultra-porous LoC to New Delhi, no attention was paid to them. The then chief minister of J&K, Farooq Abdullah, upon being asked about bomb blasts and the killings of minority Hindus, said that there was no militancy. The government maintained that the disturbances were just the handiwork of Khalistani extremists from Punjab.

The first big victory for the militants and the first death knell for India's position in Kashmir came in December 1989 after militants kidnapped Rubaiya Sayeed, the daughter of the then Union home minister and Kashmiri politician, Mufti Mohammed Sayeed. The government at the Centre buckled under and released five terrorists of the Jammu and Kashmir Liberation Front (JKLF), an organization whose men were the first to cross over to Pakistan and receive arms training.

Many Kashmiri Muslims believed that it was just a matter of weeks or months before Kashmir became 'independent'. 'It was just a euphemism for merger with Pakistan,' said a senior police officer who fought militancy in those days. Even sections of the police were sympathetic to terrorists with many believing that Abdul Ahad Guru, a doctor and an ideologue of the JKLF, would become the premier of 'Azaad Kashmir'.

After that, the police and the civil administration completely collapsed. The situation had become so cockeyed that a horde of civil servants, including senior bureaucrats, signed the JKLF's memorandum to the United Nations for a plebiscite in the state. 'I remember receiving a phone call from a civil servant who expressed his regret that he had earlier decided against becoming a signatory to the memorandum floated by Guru,' the police officer recalled.

From January 1990 onwards, the mass exodus of the minority Hindus began. Around 700 of them were killed brutally, in their homes and offices and on the streets. In a matter of a few months, most of them had left Kashmir, and had taken shelter in refugee camps in Jammu and elsewhere. In the first few years following the exodus, thousands of refugees died of depression and heat stroke and snake and scorpion bites as the camps were situated in the wilderness on the outskirts of Jammu city.

The Indian Army and paramilitary forces began fighting militants across Kashmir. Most of those who joined the militancy had little education and were incapable of putting together one coherent sentence. Photographs and videos shot in those days show a bunch of goons who suddenly gained importance because they had pistols in their hands and were wearing military fatigues.

A film on Kashmir by Gopal Sharman and Jalabala Vaidya features one such militant, Altaf Ahmed Bhat, who was among those released in exchange for Rubaiya Sayeed. The interviewer asks him what kind of music he likes. Altaf is wearing big black sunglasses that make his face look awkward. He is trying to suppress a smile. One of his friends sitting next to him mutters to him in Kashmiri that he should reply that he likes the sound of bullets.

Altaf boasts that he carried out the first rocket 'action' (attack) in Kashmir, and then goes on to list the weapons he had used. Towards the end he says in Kashmirized Hindi: *Jab se maine militancy mein kadam rakha hai, tab se mujhe ek hi music pasand hai – goliyon ki'* (Ever since I have stepped into militancy, I only like one kind of music – that of bullets).

Journalists recall how in those days this bunch of men made fools out of eager journalists working with Western media outlets who came in droves to document the 'rebellion' against the Indian state. One day, a journalist would ask his local contact, usually a stringer, to arrange an interview with a JKLF commander. So, the JKLF would ask a sympathizer from Kashmir

University who could speak in broken English to cover his face with a Palestinian scarf and pose as a JKLF commander and give an interview, since its own men knew no English. The next day, the same student would change his scarf and pose for another journalist as a commander of the Hizbul Mujahideen.

By the mid-1990s, most of those associated with the first wave of militancy were either dead or arrested or co-opted by Indian intelligence agencies. This started another dangerous game in Kashmir and is largely responsible for the mess that has continued till date: the money factor. In the name of creating assets, intelligence agencies convinced many among the militant leadership to fight elections or keep a facade of being a separatist, but secretly work for them. The Kashmiri militants learnt this game quickly. They began getting money from all quarters – from Pakistan's Inter-Services Intelligence (ISI) to India's IB. News spread fast in Kashmir of how a former militant was purportedly called to Delhi and offered Rs 50 lakh and a shopping bonanza in Delhi's Khan Market on the condition that he would fight elections. The man, too wily for Indian sleuths, took the money, returned to Kashmir and refused to fight the elections.

As the first wave of militants were either crushed

or co-opted by the Indian side, a new phenomenon emerged. Pakistan would start sending foreign terrorists to take over from the 'weak Kashmiris' and start a new wave of destruction. For the mehmaani mujahids (guest holy warriors), as the foreign terrorists began to be called in Kashmir, the Tral area in Pulwama became a sanctuary of choice. This was mostly due to its topography. Like a bowl flanked by mountains and forests, it offered unhindered access on one side to Kupwara in North Kashmir, close to the LoC, through the Dachigam–Ganderbal–Lolab belt. Terrorists used this route for years to reach South Kashmir undetected after infiltrating through the LoC. A senior police officer employed a cricket analogy to describe this pattern. 'In the north, terrorists play a one-day match and leave for the south. It is to the south that they come to play a five-day match,' he said.

On the other side of Tral, after crossing pine forests and glacial pathways, they could reach the Doda region in Jammu division, from where they could continue their journey to the other part of the LoC in the Rajouri–Poonch area.

After the waning of the JKLF in the early and mid-1990s, Tral became a hub of the Hizbul Mujahideen. The Hizbul has its roots in the Jamaat-e-Islami,

Kashmir. The Jamaat, a global movement, was founded by Maulana Syed Maududi (1903–79), who always urged his followers to see Islam as *Nizam-e-hayaat* (a code of life) and to struggle for Islamic rule. Democracy was considered *haraam* or un-Islamic.

The Jamaat in Kashmir severed its ties with the outfit in India and Pakistan and became an independent entity in 1953. The Kashmiri Jamaat's rejection of India and its focus on Islamism formed the core of the separatist movement in Kashmir. As the scholar Yoginder Sikand writes, as early as in 1980, the Jamaat declared Indian forces stationed in Kashmir to be an 'army of occupation' and appealed to Kashmiri Muslim youth to 'throw out' the Indian occupiers and establish Islamic rule in the state.

As the Hizbul Mujahideen became the dominant terrorist organization in the Valley in the 1990s, it found in Tral a comfortable base. At one point it became such a big terrorist sanctuary that the security forces started calling it Tora Bora, a reference to a mountainous area in Afghanistan that was a Taliban stronghold.

'I would say that Tral suffered from a terrible infection of the Jamaat,' said a police officer who served there in the 2000s. Tral had a high literacy rate because of the presence of several prominent madrasas. These would produce many future engineers and doctors, and also, as discreet police reports would point out, Islamist radicals, many of whom later joined terrorist ranks.

In the late 1990s, residents of Tral recall, a man called Nazir Ahmed Sofi fell out with the Hizbul. A resident of Tral's Satura village, he was a local strongman with political connections. He was one of the few people in Tral who possessed a car in those days, which he used to provide logistical support to Hizbul terrorists. And then, one day, Nazir decided to test other waters. It is not clear why, but many in Tral believe that it was because he developed serious differences with a Hizbul district commander.

In the early 2000s, as people in Tral watched, several foreign terrorists appeared in Tral's villages, on their way to the upper reaches of Tral. They would often be seen hiking through the upper reaches with long hair and beards, wearing ammunition vests over their Pathani suits. They had now begun to appear in villages, often taking rest and meals at the houses of sympathizers. In small places where everyone knows what others are up to, the police were told that it was Nazir who was bringing foreigners affiliated with the Pakistan-based Jaish as a counter to the home-grown Hizbul.

The Jaish quickly set up a big base in the upper reaches of Tral. Pakistan now wanted the Jaish to reign supreme in Kashmir and gave it all the support it needed.

An important factor that strengthened the Jaish's network in Kashmir was its access to money. In Tral, Jaish commanders spent a lot of money on people they considered to be Jaish sympathizers. In the early 2000s, local informers shared with the police the story of a Jaish commander who kept a sack of money with a villager. When the commander, a Pakistani, was killed shortly afterwards, the villager got to keep the money.

One of the men Nazir helped bring to Tral to help him establish a base there was identified as a Jaish terrorist known by his code name, Rashid Bhai. Soon, he was well entrenched in Tral and came to be known among residents as a spiritual figure. With him also came his commander Ghazi Baba, a man who would later plan the deadliest attacks in Kashmir and on India's Parliament in 2001. In 2001, the two had shifted to Tral and set up training camps for new recruits. As the Jaish's hegemony was established in Tral and its surrounding areas, the Hizbul avenged its loss of ground by killing Nazir in 2001.

In early 2003, security forces almost captured Rashid Bhai. A team of the Indian Army's Special Forces, dressed up as mujahideen, or holy warriors, and approached a local Gujjar herdsman, Akbar. He knew the terrain well, and the Jaish leadership trusted him.

Mistaking them for Rashid Bhai's freshly arrived recruits from Afghanistan, Akbar led the team to his hideout in Tral. The army attacked and destroyed it, but they could not get Rashid Bhai – he had left minutes earlier to meet a contact in a village in the neighbouring Anantnag area.

Later, the Jaish would kill Akbar and his two sons.

In the meantime, Nazir's wife had also joined the Jaish as an OGW. But a few years later, somebody had seen her coming out of an army camp, and this aroused suspicion of her becoming an informer. She was brutally killed by the Jaish. Her decapitated head shorn of hair was dropped at her village to terrorize others.

Today, Nazir's elder brother, Shamsuddin Sofi, who the police believe is around fifty years old, is one of the Jaish's commanders in Tral. Shamsuddin had started as a timber smuggler and had then become a Jaish OGW. In 2019, he joined the Jaish as an active terrorist.

By 2004, Pulwama district had around fifty active Jaish terrorists. The senior commanders always came from Pakistan, well trained in camps there. Sometimes they would miss the food they were used to and ask their Kashmiri OGWs to arrange it for them. In

2004, the police kept a watch on a small hotel on the outskirts of Tral town, where a police informer said biryani was being cooked in bulk. 'The Kashmiris did not care for biryani. So we knew some Punjabi Pakistani commander must have asked for it,' said a police officer who served in South Kashmir in those days. Eventually, it led to the busting of a Jaish hideout.

On a December morning in 2004, a police officer received a call from his superior, asking him to rush for a meeting. As the officer reached his boss's office, he was told that a dreaded Jaish terrorist, Sajjad, had been spotted at a hospital in Srinagar. A former special police officer, Sajjad had joined the Jaish after deserting the police force. An informer had tipped off the police about Sajjad's presence in the hospital where he had been admitted for the treatment of a kidney ailment.

The instructions were clear: the operation was to be conducted without creating any ruckus inside the hospital. 'If there is any doubt, drop the plan,' the police chief told his officer.

The officer took with him another policeman who had known Sajjad in his police days and could identify him. The two men, along with other policemen, reached the hospital in civilian clothes. The hospital had seventeen rooms. The officer decided to depute one man each outside these rooms; all of them wore Kashmiri loose coats called pherans, and inside them they kept their AK-47 rifles ready in case things got out of hand. Sajjad could be armed; he could have others with him.

After a while, the policeman who recognized Sajjad spotted him in one of the rooms. He and the young police officer walked calmly towards him. 'Your game is up,' his former friend told him.

While he was saying this, Sajjad reached for an AK-47 kept under his pillow. But the officer caught hold of his hand and snatched the weapon away. With the help of others, he was bundled into a waiting car and whisked away; nobody in the hospital got any time to raise an alarm.

Sajjad was kept at a secret location for forty-five days; his arrest was not made public.

'Every day I would go to him with food and have a conversation with him,' the police officer who got him would recall later.

Ultimately, Sajjad decided to cooperate. The information provided by him would prove to be vital. In the next few months, the security forces were able to eliminate most of the Jaish leadership in South Kashmir. By October 2006, out of the fifty Jaish terrorists in Pulwama, only four were left.

Sajjad, they say, runs a shop now somewhere in Kashmir and has left his old life behind. But Pulwama would remain a sanctuary for terrorists. Even as the security forces were eliminating terrorist commanders, they kept coming. It was something that a man sitting in a big complex near a railway line in Bahawalpur in Pakistan was ensuring.

~

Masood Azhar was born in 1968 in Bahawalpur, Pakistan, to a religious teacher; Masood was the third boy among his eleven children. When he was eleven, Masood was enrolled in an influential madrasa in Binori town near Karachi city. From there, he was sent for military training to a camp in Khost, Afghanistan.

But he was short and fat and totally unfit for the rigour of military training, so much so that he could not even complete the basic training. But even as he had failed there, he had impressed his handlers with his knowledge of scriptures and teaching skills. He also had an ability to make rousing speeches, which terrorist commanders of the Harkat-ul-Mujahideen (HuM), a group formed in the 1980s to fight the Soviet occupation in Afghanistan, found useful. The

HuM encouraged him to travel, and in the early 1990s, he visited twenty-five countries in Africa, Europe and elsewhere to collect funds for jihad. In this endeavour, by all accounts, he was a success.

A month after the demolition of the Babri Masjid in Ayodhya in December 1992, Azhar was sent to Pakistan-occupied Kashmir by his handlers to meet a veteran militant commander, Sajjad Afghani, who had fought alongside the mujahideen against Soviet forces. Afghani had been witness to Azhar's embarrassing performance at Khost. But now, both had been asked to travel to Kashmir to launch a new wave of jihad there. Afghani went to Dhaka first, and from there he crossed over into West Bengal, finally reaching Kashmir. Azhar reached Delhi a few days later by air from Dhaka on a Portuguese passport, masquerading as a businessman.

The immigration officer at the airport told Azhar that he did not look like a Portuguese citizen, to which he replied that he was originally from Gujarat. In Delhi, Azhar spent a night at the Ashok Hotel and then travelled to Lucknow, en route to Ayodhya.

In his sermons later, Azhar would refer repeatedly to Ayodhya. He said that the ruins of the mosque there made him very angry and that he had vowed to restore it to its former glory.

From Uttar Pradesh, Azhar reached Jammu and then finally the Kashmir Valley, where his first sermon was held at a hideout in South Kashmir's Anantnag district in 1994.

By 1994, the first wave of militancy, which began in 1988–89, had, as mentioned earlier, suffered a setback. Most of the original militants were either dead or had joined the Indian side. Added to this, the Hizbul Mujahideen, which had taken over from the JKLF as the dominant terrorist organization, was in the doldrums over the waning sentiment among many Kashmiris for *azaadi*. That day in 1994 at that secret Anantnag location, Azhar addressed two dozen armed terrorists, asking them, in the rhetorical style that was his hallmark, to launch an all-out war against India.

Azhar's stay in Kashmir proved to be extremely short. Just two days later, while travelling to another place with Afghani, their car broke down. Upon hailing an autorickshaw, he was spotted by security forces who got suspicious and arrested him.

Azhar's arrest was a big blow to his Pakistani handlers. The Indian authorities, however, had no clue how important their catch was. In custody, Azhar fooled his interrogators, who wrote in their report that the man was not involved in any terrorist activity in Kashmir.

Over the next few years, Azhar's benefactors in Pakistan made several attempts to free him. In 1994 itself, they kidnapped two foreign nationals on a trek in Kashmir, demanding the release of Azhar in exchange. Later, Omar Sheikh – who would gain infamy for the killing of *Wall Street Journal*'s reporter Daniel Pearl – was sent to India to abduct foreign nationals to secure Azhar's release. Sheikh did kidnap four tourists, but they were rescued accidentally from the outskirts of Delhi when a police party, which had gone there to investigate a case of bicycle theft, stumbled upon them in chains. It also led to Sheikh's arrest. In 1995, another attempt was made to free Azhar by taking five more foreign tourists hostage in Kashmir. But even this couldn't translate into freedom for Azhar.

In June 1999, Sajjad Afghani and other terrorists tried to escape from a Jammu prison where Azhar was also lodged. The plan failed and Afghani was killed by the prison guards.

It was in December 1999 that Pakistan eventually managed to free Azhar, when terrorists hijacked the Indian Airlines' flight IC-814 to Kandahar, Afghanistan. After a week, New Delhi freed Azhar, Omar Sheikh and a dreaded Kashmiri terrorist, Mushtaq Zargar, in exchange for the passengers of the IC-814 flight.

Zargar had a reputation for being a ruthless killer. In one of the raids, he had escaped the BSF by posing as a deranged man chewing at his own rubber slippers. Later, he would develop a special hatred for BSF personnel and was responsible for killing several of them. But in 1992, it was a BSF officer who caught him. Zargar's name was included by the Pakistanis in their list to try to project that the jihad in Kashmir was run by Kashmiris.

After his freedom, Azhar and Sheikh first went to meet Osama bin Laden and then reached Pakistan to a rousing welcome. There, in a Karachi mosque with thousands of followers, Azhar announced the formation of the Jaish-e-Mohammed (the Army of Mohammed). Its first training camp was set up at Balakot (that India targeted in 2019 after the Pulwama attack).

The Jaish did not stop at Kashmir. In December 2001, its cadre made an audacious attack on India's Parliament, bringing India and Pakistan to the brink of war.

The man who had planned that attack was, like Azhar, born in Bahawalpur. In his thirties, Rana Tahir Nadeem – he went by the nom de guerre of Ghazi Baba – was very fond of tikkas and ate them for breakfast, lunch and dinner. Like Azhar's clan, he was a follower of the Deobandi sect and was a believer in radical Islam. Some reports suggested he believed in astrology and wore precious stones. He had been sent to Kashmir as a commander of the HuM.

Ghazi Baba did not trust Kashmiris much and relied only on his own men from Pakistan to guard him round the clock. After Azhar was freed and formed the Jaish, Ghazi Baba was made the chief of the Jaish in Kashmir, while one of his close associates, Shahid Guerrilla, also joined. In that way, they became the first recruits of the Jaish. He had married a Kashmiri woman from Bandipore and they had children.

Sometime after the formation of the Jaish, Ghazi Baba shifted to Tral. It is here, investigators believe, that the plan to attack India's Parliament was hatched.

6

Getting Ghazi Baba

After the Parliament attack in December 2001 planned by Ghazi, Narendra Nath Dhar Dubey, a BSF officer serving his second tenure in Kashmir, would recall, Ghazi became hot property. Every agency inside Kashmir, and outside of it, wanted to lay its hands on him.

A month after the attack, a team of Delhi Police's Special Cell was in Kashmir, requisitioning a helicopter to conduct searches in Tral and Ganderbal, where Baba was believed to be in hiding.

Dubey had first come to Kashmir in the early 1990s, when militancy was at its peak. The BSF, along with the army, was at the forefront of fighting militancy at that time.

Dubey was sent to Kashmir with the 71 Battalion of the BSF that was formed in 1971 during the Bangladesh war. After the war, it had been stationed in Barrackpore in West Bengal and consisted mostly of

Bengali jawans. None of them, including Dubey, had ever been to Kashmir.

The battalion had its first success a few days after their deployment. A patrol party apprehended an armed Hizbul Mujahideen terrorist who was collecting money from a local market.

'The jawans had never seen a terrorist,' Dubey recalls. 'They did not know what one was supposed to look like.' They did not know what to do with a terrorist – kill him or take him into custody. And they had never seen an AK-47 rifle before. Nevertheless, they informed Dubey, who handed him over to the police after interrogating him.

In response, the BSF camp came under a rocket attack the next night. It ripped through the BSF cook's mosquito net, then hit a poplar tree, before hitting the ground. There were no casualties, but from the next day Dubey made fortifications around the campus.

Dubey remembers the initial challenges of exerting control over militancy hotbeds, especially in densely populated areas like downtown Srinagar. It was a nightmare erecting the first bunkers in these areas. 'Believe it or not, in urban areas like Jamaal Haata (near Nowhatta in downtown Srinagar), we literally asked our men to keep sandbags in the front and take position behind them to save themselves from incoming firing and stones and then put bags on other sides to create bunkers,' he recalls.

The BSF gradually began dominating these hostile areas, both in rural and urban Kashmir. It set up its small networks of informers among people. Several times it had major successes because an aggrieved housewife in a household, sick of being harassed by terrorists hiding in her house, would report them.

Once, Dubey remembers, in Kakapora, Pulwama, a woman quietly came to one of their bunkers. She said four terrorists of the Hizbul Mujahideen had taken shelter in her house and that they were harassing her daughters. The same night the BSF surrounded the house and an encounter broke out in which all four terrorists were killed.

But at times some informers would turn into a nuisance. Dubey had one such informer from Srinagar who became drunk on the little power he thought he had due to access to senior officers. All the guards knew him, and he became friendly with them. Once, while they were hanging out, he convinced one of the policemen to lend him his uniform. Then he put fake stars on his shoulders and got a picture clicked. This picture he took to his relatives to show them that he was in the police now and warned them that they should never displease him.

The man's aunt then rang up Dubey, asking him if his nephew had become a police inspector. After Dubey learnt what the man had done, he was quickly called and reprimanded. 'At times you had to mete out small punishments to such errant informers, like you do to schoolchildren,' Dubey said.

But these minor incidents apart, the BSF, with the help of officers like Dubey, was managing the counter-insurgency grid very well. 'There came a time that if you told me the colour of a gate in a particular locality, I could tell you the name of the houseowner,' he says.

In July 2001 – by this time the Jaish had replaced the Hizbul as the main terror outfit in Kashmir – Dubey, on his second posting to the Valley, was in his office when he received a call from his commanding officer. 'Come to my office immediately,' he said.

As he reached there, he found the chief of the J&K Police's Special Operations Group (SOG), Sunil Kumar, waiting for him.

Kumar told Dubey and others that he had a source who had access to Baba. The source, he revealed, was responsible for supplying rations to the Jaish commander and his men at his hideout in Ganderbal.

The plan, Kumar said, was that the source would lace Baba's food with the sedative diazepam and then a joint team of the SOG and the BSF would raid his hideout and arrest him.

The BSF began preparations for the operation. They brought out an AGS-30 automatic grenade launchers and Carl Gustaf Rocket Launchers; all of this was kept ready at their Dalgate office in Srinagar to move for the BSF's 182 Battalion stationed in Ganderbal.

But by evening the operation was called off. It looked like the SOG's mole had developed cold feet. Five months after this aborted mission Ghazi Baba's planned attack on India's Parliament was launched.

That night, as he went back home, Dubey did not know that he would be the one to ultimately 'bump off' Ghazi.

But we will come to that in a bit. For now let us turn to Dubey's experiences in Kashmir in the early 2000s which give us a valuable glimpse into the ground realities of the fight against terror. In 2002, the security forces in Kashmir faced two major challenges. Ghazi Baba had asked his men to recruit young Kashmiris who would be given a pistol each to shoot security personnel standing guard across Kashmir. These killings happened randomly across Srinagar. At the same time, the Al-

Umar Mujahideen, now run by Mushtaq Zargar from Pakistan – he was one of the terrorists released along with Masood Azhar after the IC-814 hijacking – was using young men to hurl grenades at security forces. Both these had become a big headache.

One day, Dubey watched helplessly as a grenade thrown outside his bunker in downtown Srinagar killed a fruit seller.

Soon afterwards, a source came to see him. Dubey identifies him as MM. He told Dubey that he would get into the grenade-throwing module to extract information. 'But for that I will require some hand grenade pins,' he said.

Sometimes it so happened that a novice militant would throw a grenade without taking the pin off. In such cases, the BSF would by improvisation extract the pin out of it. MM wanted the pins to prove to the kingpin that he had thrown the grenades in the past and was available for more attacks.

A few days later, he returned. He told Dubey that the entire operation was run from the kitchen of Srinagar's biggest government hospital, SMHS. 'The main guy, I don't know his name, but he sits in a room which has a wooden cupboard and a red telephone,' he said.

Dubey went there along with a couple of his

Kashmiri men in civilian clothes. After peeking through rooms for half a day, they ultimately found the room on the ground floor with the cupboard and the red telephone.

But there was no one in the room.

The next day they went again. This time they found a man who wore a leather jacket.

They brought him outside on the pretext of checking something in the OPD. MM was in the car outside and he recognized him as the main guy.

In the evening, after the general rush in the hospital ebbed, the guy was picked up. His name was Javed Ahmed.

'Mere bhi baap hain,' he said. There is someone above me.

He told Dubey that he used to meet a man at a scrap dealer's shop on Srinagar's Hari Singh High Street. The man, he said, always wore a checked suit and had a white handkerchief in his front pocket. He had no other information about him.

He said he had the shop's landline number which he had noted down in a diary that he had kept at his sister's place in Nowhatta in downtown Srinagar. Dubey's men went and recovered that diary.

The next day, Dubey went with his party and called the shop from a nearby landline. One of Dubey's men told the man at the other end of the line that he had a lot of scrap to sell. The shopkeeper gave them directions to his shop to bring it there.

As they interrogated the shopkeeper, they realized that Javed had not been dealing with him but with his relative, whom Dubey called R. The shopkeeper, they realized, had no clue about what R used to do. He said that R lived in Kupwara in North Kashmir and R's son worked as a cleaner at the Batmaloo bus stand in Srinagar and that he could take them there.

Now the risk was if they left the shopkeeper there, he could contact R and alert him. So, they detained him and R's son too. Then Dubey set out for Kupwara with a small team. They reached Kupwara at about 11 p.m.

The question now was how to operate in the night. The army intelligence in the area was under a colonel and the protocol was that he had to be intimated about any activity there. Dubey felt that he wouldn't allow them to go to R's village in the night.

Before reaching Kupwara, Dubey had seen the cement signboard with an arrow pointing towards R's village. He spoke to his boss and told him to handle this minor breach of protocol later if it were to come up in a meeting of the senior officers.

They set out for R's village. On the road leading to the village, they saw a man.

'Do you know the way to R's house?' they asked him. He gave them directions.

Once they were inside, they laid a quick cordon and barged inside. They realized R was not there.

'The first thing I spotted inside was the checked suit with a white handkerchief in its front pocket hanging from a hook,' Dubey would recall.

After searching inside, they found a VIP suitcase. They asked for the keys to it from R's wife, but she said she did not have them. They broke it open.

Inside, they found eight pistols and Rs 50,000 in cash.

Later, they received a call from Kupwara's police chief. He said he had come to know about the recovery and that they had managed to arrest R.

At the police station, Dubey was taken aback when he saw R. He realized he was the same man they had asked for directions while entering the village the previous night. R had cleanly managed to give them the slip.

They took possession of him and brought him back to their base.

R, they found out, was a deserter from the armed forces.

He knew what his arrest would mean. In those days, the general belief was that the BSF followed a catch-and-kill policy for militants.

Dubey does not comment on it, but says that they kept R for ten days, asking him about the grenade-throwing network, but not subjecting him to any torture.

'Mera bhi baap hain,' he told them. This turned out to be a man from Srinagar's Chattabal area.

The end result was that a huge consignment of arms was recovered from a field and with it the hand grenade attacks came to a halt.

Ten days later, Dubey was in his office when a sentry came. 'Someone called R says he wants to see you,' he said.

As R came in, he greeted Dubey with a crisp 'Jai Hind', like forces men do. 'I couldn't help notice that he had deserted the forces, but the forces had not deserted him,' Dubey says.

That day R and Dubey had a long conversation. R told him he was grateful that he had not killed him. 'I want to work for you,' he said.

This was dicey. Dubey knew of people who had been hired by agencies as spies, but things could get quite messy. Many spies ended up being double agents, working for the Indian authorities and for the militants side by side, putting lives in jeopardy.

But something told Dubey that he needed to trust this man.

'What do you want from me?' Dubey asked him.

R wanted a consignment of hand grenades. This was very risky. What if the grenades were misused. It could also raise very uncomfortable questions for Dubey: if an attack was carried out, it would be easy to identify a grenade issued to the BSF and this could be traced back to them. Is there no other way? he asked R. No, he replied, this is what they want.

Ultimately, Dubey took his seniors into confidence. They were already impressed with what R had brought to the table so far. R had said that a man collected such consignments near a transformer at one end of Gani Stadium in downtown Srinagar. He did this at 11 a.m. on pre-decided days. Both parties, he said, had to show a white handkerchief, after which the transaction would take place.

Does the man check what is inside the box immediately? 'No, he will just feel them. There is no time; he wants to leave as soon as possible,' R told Dubey.

Dubey hit upon a plan. With the permission of his seniors, he took out dummy grenades from his training store and packed them in a gunnysack just the way R wanted it. The dummy grenades had no explosives; they were used to train soldiers to get a feel of how to throw them.

Before 11 a.m., Dubey and his men were in place around Gani Stadium. They wore civilian clothes and hovered around. One of them stopped to urinate, another one joined some children playing with marbles. Dubey was in his car, about 150 metres from the transformer.

At sharp 11 a.m., his driver said, 'Sahib, someone is crossing the field.' Dubey could see the man was young and was walking fast.

Near the transformer he took the consignment from R and, just as he had said, felt it over the jute sack and left immediately. The route he took to exit the spot was manned by Dubey's colleague, Himanshu Gaur, who stood outside his car, pretending to change oil. As the man walked past him, Gaur caught him by his arm.

'What is in this, brother?' he asked, smiling.

'Oh nothing, just snooker balls,' the man replied.

By that time Dubey and others had surrounded him as well.

He turned out to be a graduate in aeronautical engineering from an institute in Dehradun and ran a cosmetics shop in downtown Srinagar.

'Mere se upar bhi ek hain,' he told Dubey on being questioned.

That man turned out to be a leader of the Awami Action Committee (AAC), part of the separatist conglomerate Hurriyat Conference. He even claimed to having met the then prime minister, Atal Bihari Vajpayee, as part of a delegation.

At his Zaina Kadal residence in Srinagar, as the BSF team raided it, he began to take out pictures of himself with prominent people to show how well connected he was.

But, as Dubey put him into the car, he broke down.

'Mere se upar bhi ek hain.'

He led them to a carpet seller near Soura.

Dubey remembers entering the premises and feeling nervous looking at the garden. 'I had never seen such a big garden in my life and wondered if I was doing the right thing,' he recalled. The man they were after was clearly rich and well connected.

The leader of the AAC had revealed to Dubey earlier that the man above him operated out of a Tata Sumo vehicle. As Dubey's men checked the porch, there were three cars standing there, but there was no Sumo.

It was found later in the rear of the back lawn under a tarpaulin. 'Keys, mister,' Dubey said. The man refused. Finally they broke open the car. Inside, they found blankets, bottles of mineral water and Rs 76 lakh in cash. A soldier started the car by connecting the wire and drove away with it. R had once again proved his worth.

A few months later, R came to Dubey's office again. 'I need a little help,' he said.

R told Dubey that he had a friend who had suffered injuries in a blast. His file was now stuck at the office of Srinagar's deputy commissioner, without whose consent he could not receive government compensation offered to injured victims like him.

Dubey put in a word; the file moved.

Four days later, R's friend was in Dubey's office. 'Thank you, I will be of help to you,' he said.

A few more days passed before he returned, this time with a tip for Dubey.

The friend said that the previous day he had heard two brothers in his locality, both carpenters, bitterly fighting over something. 'I don't know what, but the elder one kept telling the younger one that "this man" should not be staying here,' he said. Dubey asked him to keep an eye on the family.

A week later, he returned and told Dubey that the previous night the younger brother and his family had left for good. They left along with their belongings in an autorickshaw. He said he had noted down the number.

Dubey found that there was an auto stand nearby. Early in the morning, his men waited there. At about 11 a.m., the auto bearing the number Dubey's informer had noted down came to the stand.

Dubey's men sat in it pretending to be civilians and asked the driver to take them towards their office. They told him to drive into their base.

Dubey began to question him. After a little thought, the driver remembered picking up a family in the night. 'I dropped them in the Zoonimaar locality near Soura,' he said.

Immediately, two BSF officers, M.R. Binuchandran and Himanshu Gaur, took the driver in a civilian car to identify the house.

Once they arrived at the house, Gaur and others went inside and found a man sleeping under a blanket in the drawing room.

Binuchandran was obsessed with the idea of catching a Pakistani, Dubey recalled. 'He would come to my office and say, "Sir, *Pakistani pakadna hai* (I need to catch a Pakistani)."'

The man was shocked to see them; he had no clue that the BSF party had appeared there by chance. He turned out to be the chief of the JK Freedom Force, a lesser-known terrorist organization based in Pakistan. He was from Sialkot in Pakistan and told the BSF that he had a master's in Economics from Lahore University.

He informed Dubey that this was his second time in Kashmir. This time he had crossed over from the LoC and had been picked up from Kupwara by the carpenter's wife. She had also later carried his AK-47 rifle and Thoraya satellite phone in case someone got suspicious and decided to search him.

'That rifle was upstairs by chance. Had it been next to me, you wouldn't be alive,' he told Gaur.

As his interrogation proceeded, he opened up. Dubey was startled to realize how calm he was about their plans for Kashmir. 'See, it is not an achievement for us to kill a soldier here and there. We are looking at taking Kashmir in 2030 or 2040. We have ample time,' he told Dubey.

Dubey was dumbfounded as the man explained to him for the first time how hawala transactions work. He told them how certain businessmen in West Delhi bought electronic items from Dubai and how this was paid for by ISI agents in Dubai itself. The same amount of money, he told Dubey, the businessman would hand over to a point person of a terrorist group in Kashmir, completing the hawala transaction.

The man was also clear that he would not be left alive now. 'You know, I have never been to the Dal Lake. Please take me there once before you finish me,' he said. He also requested that he be allowed to speak to his family one last time.

~

We return now to how Dubey was able to get his prized catch – Ghazi Baba. In July 2003, the BSF was told that Prime Minister Vajpayee wanted to hold a meeting of the council of ministers in Srinagar. The security advisers wanted him to take a chopper straight from the airport to the convention centre in the VIP area of Gupkar. But Vajpayee was adamant. He said he would drive from the airport to the venue.

The meeting was fixed for 27 August. Vajpayee would drive towards the Tourist Reception Centre (TRC) in the heart of Srinagar and then head to the venue, a short distance from the TRC.

But this was a major security challenge. There could be no firing on the route. The BSF was in charge of making sure of this. The prime minister's planned visit was high profile and in the news. It was impossible to keep it under wraps. On 25 August, terrorists fired at army personnel buying chicken in a busy market, killing three of them. On 27 August, a patrolling party of the BSF's 193 Battalion was fired at, killing one jawan. The killer must have been a new recruit who wanted to do this and leave without getting caught. After firing he threw the rifle at the spot and fled by melting away in the crowd.

On the same day, the separatist conglomerate of the Hurriyat Conference called for a strike. This suited the security forces well since it meant fewer people on the roads.

The prime minister landed and as he and his convoy reached Boulevard Road, along the Dal Lake, a fidayeen attack took place in Srinagar at Hotel Greenway, just four kilometres from the prime minister's location. An ensuing encounter lasted the whole night. Three BSF personnel died while a deputy inspector general was injured.

Around the time Dubey reached his office the next day, there was a big explosion on a nearby road. He rushed there to find a big crater in the road, caused by an IED. But, thankfully, there was no casualty.

No sooner had he returned to office than the phone rang. It was Himanshu Gaur.

'Sir, rush to Shah Manzil.'

Shah Manzil was a building in downtown Srinagar which served as the BSF's strategic headquarters. Dubey thought the building had come under attack. He rushed towards that part of Srinagar.

But even as he came close to the building, he heard no gunfire.

He entered a room to find a smiling Gaur.

'Sir, we have stopped something big.'

Gaur took Dubey to another room where a young man, hardly twenty or twenty-one years old, sat on the ground, his hands tied behind his back.

Because of Vajpayee's visit, the BSF had deputed its personnel in every nook and corner of Srinagar city. In one of the narrow streets, the deployed BSF jawans saw a young man on a cycle. He got visibly nervous at the sight of the BSF. He was stopped and searched. As the jawans opened his shirt, they were shocked to see explosives tied all around his body.

He turned out to be Ansar Bhai, from Faisalabad in Pakistan. He was calm. 'I had to carry out today's attack,' he said. On being asked which organization he belonged to, Ansar shook his head. 'I am not from any tanzeem (organization),' he said. This would later turn out to be a lie.

Just as his questioning had begun, the station head officer of the area where Ansar was picked up from arrived. He told Dubey that he had been informed of the BSF picking up someone big. 'I went to the spot and collected the cycle and carried it here in my Gypsy. Congratulations,' he said sheepishly.

Every agency wanted credit for operations in Kashmir. The SHO also wanted Dubey to give him a little credit.

As Dubey looked at the cycle, something flashed across his mind. Six months earlier, he was visiting his family in Gorakhpur in Uttar Pradesh when he heard the news of an assistant commandant of the BSF getting killed in a militant attack. The officer from 193 Battalion, Mukesh Bisht, was on foot patrolling when a man on a cycle passed by and shot at him, killing him on the spot. One of his constables fired back, killing the lone terrorist as well.

Ansar was initially not willing to cooperate; he was ready to die. But the BSF had found that Pakistani terrorists could not bear it if they were stripped. Ansar had the same fear. 'Shoot me, but do not strip me, please,' he pleaded. But Dubey knew that was the only way he could get things out of him. So, he persisted.

Something else also made Ansar tell his interrogators everything. A senior police officer had a small trick that he always deployed to work on the semi-literate militants. During interrogation, the officer would tell a terrorist how 'handsome' and 'fit' he was and that if he cooperated the officer would ensure he was not only let off but also that he was made an 'important policeman' in the force. 'The dunderheads had no education to understand this was not possible at all,' said another officer who was present there.

The threat of being stripped and the lure of being made a policeman worked well on Ansar Bhai; he confessed that he was from the Jaish.

He told the interrogators that the man on the cycle they had shot six months ago was a Pakistani terrorist, Waqas Bhai. Ansar had been sent to take control of Waqas's hideout in Srinagar's Chattabal area.

'Do you know Ghazi Baba?' Dubey asked.

'Yes,' he replied.

He said he had no idea where Ghazi Baba's hideout was. 'But we speak on the wireless set twice a day, at 9.30 a.m. and 3.30 p.m.,' he said.

Ansar said when they had to meet, it was Ghazi Baba who fixed the place. He said usually it was behind the Eidgah ground in Srinagar, where prayers were offered on Eid.

This matched with what one of Dubey's trusted sources had told him. He said Ghazi Baba could sometimes be seen learning how to drive an Ambassador car in the ground.

Ansar agreed to take them to his hideout. But he said there were two other Pakistanis with him, and they might be inside during the raid. 'Be prepared for an encounter,' he told them.

At midnight, the place was raided.

In the kitchen of that house, the BSF party found a giant speaker fitted in a wall. When they removed it, they found a collapsible shutter behind which was the hideout, a full-size room. Ansar's two accomplices were not there.

Inside, they found AK-47 rifles, pistols, a measuring device to weigh explosives for preparing IEDs, fake ID cards showing them as locals, Rs 75,000 in cash and a big map of Delhi.

As they were leaving, the party picked up the houseowner, who was a clerk with the state irrigation department. He said the house had been financed by the Jaish.

About the hideout, he said it was constructed by a mason-cum-carpenter who hailed from a village in Kokarnag in South Kashmir's Anantnag district.

He knew nothing else, except that the Jaish had three similar hideouts in Tral that he was aware of.

The next morning, a BSF party raided these hideouts, but they had already been abandoned.

Dubey asked his colleagues at the 77 Battalion, stationed in South Kashmir, to apprehend the carpenter. When his name was revealed, the BSF officer in Anantnag realized he was the same man they had employed earlier to make a temple at the company headquarters.

As they kept questioning Ansar, he told them that his code name was 08. A BSF wireless operator, Gandharva Kumar, who was present there, interrupted the questioning. His commandant, D.K. Pandey, said that if Ansar was 08, it meant he was the deputy of Ghazi Baba, whose code name was 39.

In those days the BSF kept all radio sets recovered from terrorists in a room at the same frequency and operators listened to the chatter day and night in shifts. From this chatter they had picked up the code names for Ansar, Ghazi and others.

Gandharva Kumar, who was an expert in local

interception, had heard terrorists calling 39 several times and saying *'Murga tapka diya hain'* (The chicken has been killed) every time they murdered a soldier.

Dubey convinced Ansar to call 39 at his usual time of 3.30 p.m. and try to extract information from him.

But as soon as they switched on the set, they heard Ghazi speaking to someone else. Ansar recognized Ghazi's voice immediately. 'This is Masterji,' he said, using the name they called Ghazi out of reverence.

As they listened on, Ghazi told the unknown man on the other side that 08 (Ansar) had been missing since yesterday. 'Be alert,' he said.

Now Ansar was of no use to them. Ghazi Baba wouldn't be honest with Ansar as he was already suspecting Ansar had been caught by security forces and that they could be listening in.

The carpenter was brought to the base. He said he was employed by the Jaish to make such hideouts. But he said he was always blindfolded before he would be taken to construct these houses, most of them in Old Srinagar. He said he had made at least twelve such hideouts across Srinagar.

'But I can tell you the location of one hideout,' he said.

Adil Dar and Umar Farooq after recording Dar's video.

Left: Dar and Farooq resting at Insha Jan's house.
Right: Umar Farooq with his lover Insha Jan.

Top: Lamboo, Umar Farooq and Hanjila Jihadi.

Centre: Umar Farooq at the Jaish launchpad, just across the international border in Jammu.

Bottom: Rouf Asgar Alvi, the operational head of the Jaish with his brother, Ammar Alvi.

The Maruti Eeco car parked at Shakir Bashir's house.

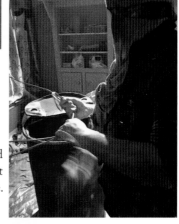

Making the improvised explosive device (IED) at Shakir Bashir's house.

Jaish terrorist Mudasir Khan, who procured gelatine sticks for the blast.

Jaish overground worker (OGW) Shakir Bashir, who sheltered Umar Farooq at his house and later drove Adil Dar to the spot.

Name: shakir bashir
s/o Bashir ah magray
R/O Hajibal kakapora pulwama
ph: 9018837008

Screenshot of the WhatsApp chat between Umar Farooq and his uncle where he discusses expenditure incurred in the Pulwama operation.

Jaish terrorist Sajjad Ahmed Bhat, who arranged the car used in the bombing.

Umar Farooq's body
after the March 2019
encounter.

Umar Farooq's brother,
Usman Haider.

Top: Ashiq Ahmed Nengroo, who transported Umar Farooq and many other Jaish terrorists from Jammu to Srinagar.

Bottom left: Jaish OGW Waiz-ul-Islam, who used his Amazon account to buy, among other things, aluminium powder for terrorists.

Bottom right: Noor Tantray, who revived the Jaish in Kashmir after his release from the parole.

Left: Jaish commander Ghazi Baba at one of the Mughal gardens in Kashmir. This photo was recovered from an album in his hideout.

Below: Ghazi Baba's body after the encounter in his hideout.

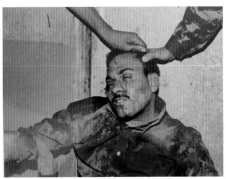

Fake government IDs used by Ghazi Baba and his close aide Rashid Bhai.

Ghazi Baba's Kashmiri wife, Sadia.

BSF officer Narendra Nath Dhar Dubey (left) showing weapons
recovered from Ansar Bhai's hideout.

He told the BSF that once he had been brought to construct a hideout in the Noorbagh area in Old Srinagar. While working, he had come out to smoke and had seen the outdoors.

Dubey put him in a Santro car with his men and took him to identify the house.

Once the house was identified, a big meeting of police officials took place at Dubey's office. Some advised him to raid the place right after midnight, but he wanted to do it in the wee hours of the morning. After they were gone, Dubey went to sleep at his house at around midnight. He was woken up at around 3 a.m. by his colleagues.

'Sir, it is time to go.'

The day was 30 August. Dubey's wife was fasting for Teej. They had plans to go to the Shankaracharya temple. But now all this would have to wait till he returned.

If he returned at all, Dubey remembers telling himself.

As he was leaving, a young BSF jawan from Rajasthan, Balbir Singh, requested that he be taken along. He was not part of Dubey's team. But Dubey took him along anyway. As they left, Dubey's wife handed a jacket to Balbir for Dubey.

By this time the BSF had laid a cordon in the area. Dubey took with him nine men, including his colleagues C.P. Trivedi, Himanshu Gaur and Binuchandran.

They decided to get down a mile before and walk to the house. 'I asked everyone to tread softly so that their boots wouldn't make noise and also to keep the rifle chains from jangling,' he says.

As he reached the spot, Dubey was livid. The advance party of the BSF had laid siege around the wrong house! In two minutes, Dubey corrected this. As the right house was cordoned off, Dubey saw that someone on the house's top (third) floor had switched on a light and then switched it off.

'The light shouldn't have been switched on. And if it was, then it shouldn't have been switched off,' he recalled. This was clearly a signal.

Binuchandran kicked open the gate. Dubey checked his watch; it was 4.10 a.m.

It was a typical Kashmiri house. There were rooms on both sides of a corridor. On the ground floor there were a few elderly people sleeping in the room on the right side. They checked the room on the left side and found a few more sleeping there. They were woken up and asked to join the others in the room on the right.

As they were climbing the stairs to the first floor, they saw a woman with a toddler coming down. No words were exchanged; it was assumed that she would join the others on the ground floor.

There was no one on the first and second floors. The rooms were filled with the usual household items and there were thick quilts and cushions in each room.

On the third floor, the house's top floor where Dubey had spotted someone switching the light on and off, there was nothing much except a few cushions and wall-to-wall carpeting. Against one wall was a dressing table of sorts with a mirror. Binu, remembers Dubey, picked up a comb and began combing his hair.

Dubey was getting frustrated. There was nothing here. He asked his men to bring the carpenter who was in a car on the road below. When he was brought, he said nothing except one word: sheesha (mirror).

At this moment, there were five men in the small room, the rest were on the stairs. Binu lifted his rifle and hit the mirror.

What Dubey remembers of the next five minutes is this: there was a deafening explosion as soon as the mirror fell down and a burst of bullets from inside the room that the mirror was hiding. Balbir Singh took the first hit and was dead. A hand grenade thrown from inside exploded and its splinters claimed two fingers of one of the BSF soldiers, Neelkamal.

Dubey looked down after the grenade explosion. His right hand was nearly severed from his arm, but he felt no pain. He picked up his rifle with his left hand and fired inside, a total of fourteen rounds. Then another hand grenade came and landed at his feet. He kicked it back inside. As he did this he saw a man in a blue shirt lying motionless face down inside the room.

Dubey's colleagues Trivedi and Binu were somewhere inside the smoke-filled room and he had no idea what had happened to them. It was around this time that a Kashmiri constable from Anantnag evacuated him.

'I just told him that my blood group is B +ive,' Dubey recalls.

In the confusion, the two found themselves alone in a vehicle with no guards on the way to SMHS Hospital. 'I saw that there was an SLR (self-loading rifle) in the vehicle. If need be, I would have used that,' he said.

Dubey, of course, had no idea about the extent of his injuries. A bullet had hit his stomach and perforated his intestines. When the doctors told him that, he asked to be taken to the army's base hospital.

By that time, the BSF's own ambulance and medical staff had arrived and they took him to the army hospital.

'On my way I was thinking that Trivedi and Binu must have died.'

Back home, Dubey's wife had no clue what had happened. Dubey's commandant knew, and so did the commandant's wife, a friend of Dubey's wife, but nobody had the heart to tell her. It was widely believed that Dubey would not survive.

Dubey lived on the first floor of a building which had a dispensary on the ground floor. That morning when Dubey's wife stepped out on to her balcony she spotted a few men with minor injuries being brought inside, presumably to the dispensary. She recognized them as the ones who had accompanied her husband just a few hours ago. Her heart sank. It was at that moment that the phone rang. By this time, she was a bundle of nerves.

On the line was a senior army officer, Colonel Pachouri, who had come to know the Dubey family and had recently had them over for dinner. He had visited Dubey in the hospital and had called her to tell her that her husband would be okay.

But coming back to the bloody encounter, earlier that morning around the time it was about to start, an army unit operating in Sumbal, Kashmir, had intercepted a wireless communication between two men. One of them said that he had been caught in a cordon and it looked like the security forces had laid it for him. The unit wasted no time and called a senior official of the IB. 'Are you aware of any operation happening in downtown Srinagar?' they asked. The IB had no clue. 'We are sure that the man we caught on radio is Ghazi Baba,' they said.

Within minutes, hordes of forces from other agencies had reached the spot of the encounter. If it were indeed Ghazi Baba, they would all want a share in the pie.

Meanwhile, inside the house where the encounter was taking place, Binuchandran and C.P. Trivedi were still alive, not sure of how to proceed further.

After a few minutes, they saw a candlelight. It was the woman they had seen coming down the stairs with the child as they had been climbing up. When she saw them alive, she silently turned back.

In the candlelight they saw the body of the man in the blue shirt. Now, the question was how to get out. They could not risk going down the stairs. They feared that there might be a hideout beneath the stairs and they may come under fire from terrorists hiding inside.

Binu decided to climb out of a window and use the wooden frame that runs along the tin roof of traditional Kashmiri houses to go down gradually. As he stepped out, the forces laying siege around the house mistook him for a terrorist and fired at him. A bullet hit his holster and his pistol fell down. Minutes later, C.P. Trivedi also came out on the roof.

But even then someone was firing from inside and throwing grenades. On the ground, Nitish Kumar, then superintendent of police, South Srinagar, was trying to save Binu and Trivedi. Police cars were sent to the ground just below where Binu was hanging by the roof so that he could jump into one of them. But in the process, several police drivers were injured by grenade splinters from inside. Finally, Binu jumped, but was seriously injured in the process. Luckily, by that time the firing had stopped from inside and Trivedi could land without injury on a mattress laid by the police.

Later, the security forces barged into the house. They found a body on the first-floor balcony. The body upstairs of the man in the blue shirt was identified as that of none other than Ghazi Baba. The man on the balcony turned out to be his close associate Rashid Bhai. He had tried to escape in an injured state from the window and had died in the process. It is he whom Nazir Sofi had earlier brought to Tral. And now both he and his commander were dead.

The woman with the child turned out to be Ghazi's Kashmiri wife, Sadia. She later managed to flee to Pakistan along with her daughter. Last heard, she had remarried another prominent jihadi associated with the Jaish.

Dubey was operated on; a bullet was lodged in his abdominal viscera. They had to remove large parts of his intestines. The doctors realized that it would be too risky to try and take the bullet out, so they left it there. His hand was somehow stitched back, but it took years for it to be somewhat functional.

Later, when they checked his uniform, they saw that a commendation badge he was wearing was hit by a bullet, deflecting it. Otherwise, the bullet would have ripped apart his heart. There were several other holes on the sides of his uniform, caused by bullets passing through it.

A year later, in 2004, a police officer attending Nitish Kumar's wedding remembers two men limping towards the podium, their shoulders hunched and jaws clenched in pain as they walked. These were Dubey and Binu, making it a point to attend their friend's wedding.

Dubey had to spend years in and out of the intensive care unit of Delhi's All India Institute of Medical Sciences before he could have a semblance of a normal life.

7

The Dwarfish Merchant of Death

Around 800 kilometres away, on the same evening as the encounter that killed Ghazi Baba and Rashid Bhai, a man of a diminutive figure who would go on to create the network of foot soldiers used by the Jaish to carry out the Pulwama attack, was on a mission. But, unknown to him, his details had been passed on to the Delhi Police by their counterparts in Kashmir.

That evening a few men waited quietly on the Qutab Road near Delhi's Azadpur fruit market. In front of them stood a truck bearing the number JK030153. At about 7.45 p.m., the diminutive figure approached the truck and began speaking to the driver and another man sitting next to him.

The waiting men rushed towards the truck and apprehended the three men.

The waiting men were from Delhi Police's Special Cell and were working on a specific tip-off that a truck bearing this number was carrying ammunition. The truck had been located by one of their spotters at 2 p.m. that day. They had been looking for it for two days.

In the rear of the truck three wooden boxes with 'Irfan Fruit' written on them were found. Two of them contained pears. But when the third one was opened, the police found ten hand grenades and one under-barrel grenade launcher.

The dwarfish man was Noor Mohammed Tantray from Tral, also known as Noor Trali.

He told the interrogators that he was carrying the ammunition on behalf of Rashid Bhai – who was killed on the morning of Tantray's apprehension – and was supposed to hand it over to a man called Aslam from Uttar Pradesh's Sikandrabad area. A police team waited for Aslam to arrive at the spot which Tantray had revealed in his interrogation. It happened to be outside Indraprastha Park on Delhi's Outer Ring Road.

At 10.45 p.m., a Maruti car with the number DL3C-N8749 appeared at the spot. Two men stepped out of it.

When the police confronted the men, they opened fire, which was returned, claim the police. Both the men from the Maruti car were injured and died on their way to the hospital. One of them was Aslam, while the other was identified as a resident of Khushab in Pakistan. One AK-56 rifle, some other ammunition and Rs 2 lakh in cash were recovered from the car. The police claimed that they too were Jaish operatives.

Tantray had stayed with an acquaintance in a locality near Azadpur. These premises were also raided and computers, Nokia phones, ten channel cordless phones and Rs 20 lakh in cash were recovered. Tantray revealed that he had received this money through a hawala operator in Delhi who had received it on instructions from a man in Dubai.

Upon Tantray's confession, he was led to Mirza Guest House in Delhi's Jama Masjid area where records revealed that he had stayed eleven times. He had also stayed at Seema Lodge in Chawri Bazar. He was in touch with one telephone number in Pakistan, 00925881046442, and satellite phone numbers 008821651150682 and 00821651150059.

In 2011, a special court in Delhi sentenced Tantray to life imprisonment, calling him a 'merchant of death'.

~

Tantray was born in Dar Ganai Gund village in Tral in 1970. In Tral, people who knew him from his childhood said he had developed some deformity early on and could grow only a little over four feet tall. He also walked with a limp. He began work as an apprentice in a tailoring shop and learnt the trade. Tantray apparently turned to religion to compensate for his physical shortcomings. He soon became a spiritual figure of sorts and was a big draw for people, especially in rural areas. People would come to him and beseech him to use his spiritual powers to find them a lost cow or to give them an amulet to ward off bad luck. He came to be known as Pir Baba.

In the 1990s, at the peak of the insurgency in Kashmir, Tantray joined the Hizbul Mujahideen where he worked till 1998. Soon afterwards, he came in touch with Shahid Guerrilla in South Kashmir's Anantnag town. As mentioned earlier, Guerrilla, who operated from Anantnag's Kokarnag area, was close to Ghazi Baba. Both Ghazi and he had been recruited to join the Jaish by Masood Azhar shortly after the Jaish's founding. Tantray was impressed with Guerrilla and offered him his services.

Guerrilla would later confide to his friends that he was unsure of Tantray at first. 'My first thoughts were that a man who needed help himself, how could he have helped us,' he told them. But soon, Guerrilla saw that Tantray could be an asset. Tantray had travelled across the Kashmir Valley and knew people sympathetic to radical Islamists in every corner. He also travelled far to offer people his spiritual services. For weeks, Guerrilla travelled with him to far-flung places and saw that people opened their doors for him.

Once Guerrilla was convinced, he introduced Tantray to Ghazi Baba. He had briefed Ghazi Baba about how Tantray knew a wide spectrum of people across the Valley. Also, because he had dwarfism and walked with a limp, security forces did not suspect him of being a terrorist. He was immediately given the task of ferrying men and ammunition. For this purpose, a car was also arranged for him. As one of his terrorist accomplices would recall later, 'After he took over, nobody complained of shortage of ammunition throughout the Valley.' Many times, he took terrorists to new areas for reconnaissance.

The funding for such activities came from a complex hawala system. For this, Tantray travelled frequently to Delhi and Mumbai.

Shortly after Masood Azhar's release from prison and the founding of the Jaish, there was jubilation in the terrorist ranks all over. Tantray told Ghazi Baba that he wanted to go to Pakistan and meet Azhar and other jihadi leaders. Initially, he was not taken seriously. Crossing the LoC requires a certain amount of physical fitness, which Tantray did not possess. But as he persisted, it became tough to say no to him, his friends would later recall.

Sometime shortly afterwards, in April 2000, Tantray received a man at his residence who gave him instructions to travel to Poonch in the Jammu region, a town along the LoC. There he joined a group of terrorists. It was a difficult journey. Tantray had to be carried several times as he could not walk and slowed down the party. But at last, he reached Pakistan-occupied Kashmir where he was received well. A day later, he met Masood Azhar.

Later, Tantray would claim to senior police officials that he had attended the Jaish's Rehmania camp near the Bagram airbase in Afghanistan. He said he had also visited the Al-Farouq training camp in Khost, Afghanistan, from where the top cadre of Al-Qaeda passes out. It is this camp that some top Islamist terrorists who have wreaked havoc all over the world have been to, including the four 9/11 hijackers.

After six months, it was time to return. The Jaish asked Tantray to retrace his path. But this time as his friend would recall, he said he wanted to cross back all the way to the Valley on foot.

As luck would have it, Ghazi Baba's aide Rashid Bhai was in Pakistan at that time and was returning to Kashmir. So Tantray accompanied him. Their group crossed the LoC into Poonch and from there they took a mountain route to Doda and proceeded to Tral.

The journey took several weeks. The group carried medicine and arms and dry rations like rice and pulses and animal fat which they used to cook their food. After dropping Tantray, Rashid Bhai went to his hideout in Dooru, Anantnag.

Once he was back, Tantray helped Ghazi Baba to shift his base to South Kashmir from North and Central Kashmir. Before this, most terrorist hideouts in South Kashmir used to be in the upper reaches. But with Tantray's help, the Jaish was able to create several safe hideouts in towns. Tantray also made hideouts for Ghazi Baba in the heart of Srinagar city (Ghazi had been hiding in one such hideout when he was killed). Tantray is believed to have bought land and under-construction houses of friends and acquaintances and turned them into safe houses. This shifting to South Kashmir helped Ghazi Baba create several training camps in the forest areas, especially in the upper reaches of Tral.

Four years after his conviction in 2011, Tantray, in a surprise move, was shifted from Delhi's Tihar Jail to the Central Prison in Srinagar.

As the Jaish would claim later in its mouthpiece, *Al-Qalam*, the terrorist leadership had 'total control' over the jail. Here, Tantray became a leader of prisoners. He was revered, partially because of his track record in the world of terrorists and also because of his spiritual aura. Here, his terrorist friends were able to reconnect with him.

The Jaish would claim later that in 2015, Tantray sent a message to its leadership through a courier that he wanted to apply for parole. He reportedly told them that after the 2014 floods in Kashmir, the authorities were lax in issuing parole. He sent two men to them and said that they should be sent across to Pakistan to get 'saamaan' (stuff) for him, which he said he would need once he was set free.

According to the Jaish, some officials working for Indian security agencies had approached Tantray in jail, asking him to help them. They said if he agreed, they would make sure his parole application went through. The Jaish says, 'We do not know how the enemy forgot all wounds inflicted upon them by Maulvi sahib (Tantray). Or maybe they had not forgotten but had wrongly imagined that incarceration had broken Maulvi sahib.'

Tantray readily agreed to work for the Indian security agencies, the Jaish claims. He wanted to get out of jail and be a part of the jihadi network again. On their part, the Jaish said that they trusted him so much that even if they spotted him travelling with Indian Army generals in a helicopter they would still know that he was working for them. Their trust was not misplaced. Tantray would fool the Indian agencies for the next couple of years. During this period, he made some startling revelations. He claimed that one of the terrorists responsible for the October 2001 assembly attack in Srinagar named Raja, who hailed from Karachi, Pakistan, had managed to escape that day and was one of those killed two months later during the Parliament attack. He also named two Jaish terrorists who were involved in the planning of the IC-814 plane hijacking. According to Tantray, one of them was a man of Assamese origin, Yusuf Bhai, who later became the chief instructor at the Jaish's Balakot camp. The other was a Pakistani with the code name Arsalan, who sneaked into Kashmir two months before the

October 2001 assembly attack. Afterwards he joined Ghazi Baba in Tral and then later shifted to another base in Srinagar's Chanapora area. Tantray claimed it was from this hideout that Afzal Guru picked up Arsalan and brought him to Delhi for the execution of the Parliament attack. Arsalan was one of the five terrorists killed inside Parliament that day.

In September 2015, after staying in prison for twelve years, Tantray was finally set free. He instructed the Jaish people not to visit his house under any circumstances because it would be under watch.

From the security establishment he had a handler he would keep giving information to, the Jaish claims, but this was mostly about men the Jaish wanted to cut loose. The Jaish called the year 2016 a 'fun year'.

The 'fun' had actually begun after the BJP's alliance with the People's Democratic Party (PDP) in 2015. The PDP had won its first election in 2002. The victory was ascribed by intelligence agencies to Mehbooba Mufti, the daughter of the PDP chief, Mufti Mohammed Sayeed. They reported that Mehbooba had gone to the Jamaat in South Kashmir and assured its leaders of patronage if the PDP came to power. Remember, the Hizbul Mujahideen has its roots in the Jamaat.

In 2015, after it came back to power with the BJP,

Mufti lost no time to reward his Jamaat friends. The first thing he did was to ask the police to halt anti-militant operations. He also ordered the release of Massarat Alam, a radical Islamist who had been in jail since 2010. He also had plans to release Qasim Faktoo, the Hizbul Mujahideen terrorist and husband of separatist leader Asiya Andrabi.

On 16 April 2015, soon after his release, Alam organized a big reception for his mentor, Syed Ali Shah Geelani, who was returning from Delhi where he had shifted for the winter. In a huge rally that passed by the director general of police's office in Srinagar, the crowd shouted: *'Pakistan se kya paigaam? Kashmir banega Pakistan'* (What is the message from Pakistan? Kashmir will turn into Pakistan) and *'Jeeve, jeeve Pakistan'* (Long live Pakistan). The rally boosted the spirit of youngsters who had grudgingly accepted that *azaadi* was a mirage.

As the separatist elements got emboldened by the leadership in the state, police officers became frustrated. 'I would arrest a stone pelter, only to watch him be set free after ten days. Sometimes we got so frustrated that we would ask the judge to at least book him on charges of eve-teasing so that he stayed in jail for slightly longer,' said an officer.

It was these circumstances that enabled the Jaish to make fresh inroads into Kashmir with renewed vigour. In November 2016, the Jaish attacked an army camp in Nagrota, Jammu. When summoned for information, Tantray is believed to have told his handler that it was not done by the Jaish – and his handler believed him. Meanwhile, he kept at his work for the Jaish, giving shelter to its men.

In the beginning of 2017, a senior Jaish commander from Pakistan, Mufti Waqas, entered Kashmir along with his group. Tantray's brother, who was later arrested, would claim to the NIA interrogators that Tantray had made Waqas do a little self-grooming and wear formal clothes and taken him to a senior police officer in Kashmir, fibbing to him that he would also work for the police.

Waqas, claimed the Jaish, would later tell the leadership in Pakistan that he felt in Kashmir as if he were visiting his khala's (aunt's) house. (He was later killed in an encounter with the security forces in March 2018.)

Around the same time, there were multiple grenade attacks in South Kashmir. The Jaish did not take responsibility for them to confuse the security agencies. But the police had come to know from other sources that this was indeed the Jaish's handiwork. A junior handler called Tantray and told him that he needed to deliver on his promise of sharing information about the Jaish. Tantray told him that he would get back to them. He did, giving the handler names of Jaish OGWs who he knew were already exposed.

Tantray was devious. He used his connection with his handler to move around without hassles. Before he had to leave, he would inform his handler that he was going towards a particular area for his work. The Jaish claims he was even allowed to keep a pistol with him.

But the agencies were getting restless. A man like Tantray should have been able to help them net some big terrorists by now. Tantray also knew that his days of fooling the agencies were limited, so he told his commanders that he might have to openly go back to being a 'mujahid'. The Jaish leadership asked him to continue for as long as he could. And at any point if he sensed danger, he could come out in the open as a mujahid without consulting them.

On 15 July 2017, security forces attacked a Jaish camp in the Satura jungles in Tral. Three terrorists were killed. Two of them were from Tral. The third one was a Pakistani. It was an operation in which the army's para commandos were dropped from a chopper for the final assault.

Tantray turned into an open Jaish terrorist right afterwards. By this time, however, he had fooled his handlers for almost two years.

The agencies went after him hard, conducting raid after raid in the entire Pulwama district, including Tral, but Tantray had moved to Srinagar. Taking agencies into confidence and then betraying them had been Tantray's speciality. In 2003, just before he was arrested by the Delhi Police, Tantray had even visited the headquarters of the BJP in Delhi, getting himself a membership form. He wanted to use his membership to get access to senior leaders whom he could later assassinate. Sources would reveal that before his parole in 2015, Tantray had even approached a central investigation agency, asking them to utilize his 'services' to counter terrorism in Kashmir. As Tantray finally became an open Jaish terrorist, it left the agencies red-faced.

From his Srinagar base, Tantray started planning an attack on the BSF campus in Humhama. The entire recce was done by him. A few weeks later, when he was sure that he had understood the area, he gave the go-ahead for the attack. On 3 October 2017, three fidayeen met him and spent their final hours with him.

Later, at the BSF camp, the three terrorists rushed in different directions, one towards the mess inside, one towards the canteen area. The third one was spotted by a sentry at the gate and shot. The second one was killed after being engaged in the mess building while the last one was contained in the administration block and later killed.

One assistant sub-inspector, Braj Kishore Yadav, lost his life in the attack.

After Humhama, Tantray began planning another big attack. This time he chose the CRPF camp in Lethpora, Pulwama. He began preparations for that, doing a recce of the site again. This time, he wanted the fidayeen to be able to inflict severe damage to human life. On the evening of 25 December 2017, Tantray accompanied a Pakistani terrorist, Hanzila Bhai, to Pulwama's Samboora area. The Jaish's commanders had cautioned him not to go there, as they felt the area was under surveillance. But Tantray went there anyway – it is not clear why.

Just 50–60 metres before his hideout, an associate of his would later write in *Al-Qalam*, Tantray saw some people coming. Tantray, according to what Hanzila told the Jaish leadership later, told him that these were 'bad people'.

The same night, his safe house was raided. The whole house was bathed in searchlights so that there was no chance of escape. Tantray realized that his end had come. 'I cannot run,' he reportedly told Hanzila, 'but you go, I will cover you.' Tantray was killed in the raid.

Five days after his death, the Jaish began publishing a serialized eulogy for Tantray in *Al-Qalam*. 'People of his height are generally used by this world for entertainment,' the first chapter read. 'You must have seen dwarves used in hotels to open (doors for) guests and to entertain guests. They perform tricks on the roadside to lure customers to some petrol pump. But with the same deformity Maulvi sahib (Tantray) made India writhe in pain for twenty-five years.'

The third chapter talked about how Afzal Guru, hanged in the Parliament attack case, was trained by Tantray himself. 'It is he (Tantray) who fulfilled that task that is a nightmare for India's warriors,' it said, referring to the Parliament attack. 'All things required for the operation were provided by Noor (Tantray) only,' it further read.

It observed that even days after his death, Tantray's house continued to attract people as if they were coming to a fair.

~

On 31 December 2017, a few days after Tantray was killed, the CRPF camp at Lethpora came under attack by three terrorists. Just before the Pulwama attack, the NIA had managed to arrest a man called Fayaz Ahmed Magray, who they found out was one of the key conspirators of the attack on the Lethpora CRPF camp. Remember, this was the attack that Tantray was planning shortly before he was killed on 25 December 2017 in a raid. The attack was a tribute of sorts to Tantray and was carried out to avenge his death. As mentioned earlier, Mudasir Khan, the now-dead resident of Tral whom many believed to be the mastermind of the Pulwama suicide attack, had come under the authorities' scanner after the same Lethpora attack.

The NIA investigation revealed that it was Magray who had taken Tantray towards the Lethpora CRPF camp to carry out a recce around the second week of December. Tantray, who wore a burqa to hide his identity, was accompanied by Sajjad Bhat, the absconding man who owned the car used in the Pulwama attack and who later, after the attack, formally joined the Jaish's fidayeen squad and was given the code name Afzal Guru.

After Tantray was killed, on 28 December 2017,

Magray was called by Mudasir Khan to attend a meeting where Sajjad Bhat and the Pakistani terrorist Abdul Shakoor were present. It was decided then that the camp would be attacked to take revenge for Tantray's killing.

Magray suggested that a heavy vehicle be used for the attack to easily break into the camp. Here, Sajjad Bhat told them about two Kashmiri boys who would attack the camp along with Shakoor; he said Tantray himself had motivated and readied the two for this attack.

In the murky world of insurgency, security agencies and terrorist groups often fish from the same pool to strengthen themselves. While terrorist groups look for young men who have shown some 'promise' (that is, who are stone pelters) to turn them first into OGWs and then into active militants, the police also try to turn some of them into informers. Many times they give them valuable information, but sometimes militants also take advantage of this to stay above suspicion while carrying on working for terrorist groups.

Magray, the NIA realized, had done something similar. Just before the attack, he had contacted a police officer and shared with him information about an impending terrorist attack but misled him completely on where it would take place.

As a result, when the attack took place on the CRPF camp, the police were caught unawares; their attention was elsewhere.

From the encounter site, security personnel recovered a pocket diary with a red cover, belonging to the Pakistani terrorist Shakoor. It contained, among other vital information, a rough map of the CRPF camp, including details of sentry posts and the residential complex. It also had some personal jottings of Shakoor. Some of them give us a glimpse into the mindset of Islamist extremists like Shakoor who are mentally prepared for death.

Main namaz pad raha hoon taaki kafir ko maarne ki jo dil mein bechaini hai woh zaroor kam ho (I am offering prayers so that my restlessness for killing infidels ebbs).

Khalid ibn al-Waleed hum Jaish ke jaan nisaaron ka kal roz jannat ke darwaze par intezaar kar raha hoga (Khalid ibn al-Waleed [a military commander of the Prophet Mohammed who helped him in Islamic expansion] will be waiting for us Jaish daredevils tomorrow at the gates of heaven).

~

It was becoming apparent that the men who attacked the Lethpora CRPF camp to avenge the death of Tantray – Sajjad Bhat and Mudasir Khan – also played a leading role in the Pulwama suicide attack. But a coherent picture was not so easy to draw. These men seemed like foot soldiers, not the masterminds.

Tantray's brother, Nisar, had fled Kashmir in February just before the Pulwama attack and hidden himself in the UAE. At the request of Indian authorities, the UAE extradited Nisar Tantray on 31 March 2019 in a special aircraft; he was taken into custody by the NIA right afterwards. Nisar told NIA officials that Mudasir Khan had informed him about their plans to attack a convoy in Pulwama. After the attack, he said, he had spoken to a senior Jaish commander, Qari Yasir, and asked him why another man from Tral, Yawar Ahmed Najar, was not used for the suicide attack. Yasir told him that the Jaish was not sure about his driving skills and hence had chosen Adil as their bomber.

Najar, he revealed, would have been the next suicide bomber. But, as the Pulwama attack evoked a strong response from India, the Jaish leadership decided not to carry out another strike immediately. We saw the cancelling of the next attack in the message exchange between the burly man of Bahawalpur and the Sindhi ajrak topi–wearing commander. Who were these two men? And how would the investigators get to them? They were the true masterminds of the Pulwama attack – not Mudasir Khan or Sajjad Bhat. It is through them that the trail would take us to Pakistan.

But for the moment the Sindhi topi wearing–commander at least was not on the NIA's radar.

~

On 17 June 2019, Sajjad Bhat – who had been underground since the Pulwama attack – was stuck along with one other terrorist in a two-storeyed house in the Marhama area of Anantnag district after a cordon was laid by a joint team of the CRPF, the army and the police at around 1 a.m. They tried to break the cordon, firing incessantly, resulting in the death of an army soldier.

At 5.55 a.m. the next day, the firing began again. At 11.30 a.m., Bhat tried to flee by escaping out of the two-storeyed house they were caught in. He was killed immediately.

Sajjad was dead. Mudasir was long dead. Nisar's information hadn't been that helpful.

There still wasn't anything known about the conspiracy or how the whole operation was put together.

After each death, police or other security officials would appear on TV, claiming that the mastermind had been killed. But no chain could be established that could connect the operation to Pakistan.

8

The Mobile Phone

The NIA investigators were hitting roadblock after roadblock. Jaish terrorists were getting killed all around Balwal. But there was no breakthrough in sight.

Balwal decided to investigate attacks perpetrated by the Jaish after the Pulwama attack. But there was not much he could find out. Most encounters happened when terrorists hiding in some house were trapped. Apart from arms and ammunition, they hardly left anything else. Balwal hoped that at some point one of them might leave a diary or a note behind, which might give him a clue about Pulwama. But after examining dozens of such cases, his quest came a cropper.

In the general elections of May 2019, the BJP had got a whopping majority. Even as the NIA teams were groping in the dark, signals had begun to appear from the new government that something major was afoot in Kashmir. By July end, it looked to many Kashmiris as if some military conflict with Pakistan was going to take place. CRPF officers who had served in Kashmir earlier and had been transferred later received many calls from Kashmiris they had known during their tenure.

'Sir, I think Delhi is sending its fighter planes to bomb us,' said one alarmed Kashmiri to an officer posted in faraway Bastar, Chhattisgarh.

Some believed that a military operation would be launched to flush out some major Jaish commanders who had managed to sneak into the Valley.

On the midnight of 4–5 August, internet and telephone services in the entire state were snapped. The next day, the government announced the abrogation of Article 370 and turned J&K into a union territory.

It was a big step. The separatist machinery and even the mainstream political leaders in Kashmir had believed that this Rubicon would never be crossed. But it was, and as government sources would affirm later, the resolve to remove Article 370 got its final booster on the day Adil Dar rammed his car into the CRPF convoy in Pulwama.

Before the abrogation hundreds of potential troublemakers were picked up and put in jail as a precautionary measure. One of the men arrested at that time happened to be the owner of the house in

Sathu Kalan locality in Nowgam area where on 29 March 2019 two Pakistani terrorists had been killed in an encounter. The police suspected the owner of the house to be somehow involved in militant activities. His questioning began, but it did not reveal much.

In the beginning of October, Balwal visited the Nowgam police station as part of his efforts to learn about attacks and encounters involving the Jaish. For the police, the big fish that got eliminated on 29 March was a Jaish terrorist called Kamran. As Balwal looked at the photo of the two slain terrorists, something struck him about the other terrorist killed with Kamran. In his twenties, the man wore a black Adidas jacket with black pants and black shoes. He appeared well groomed, unlike most terrorists. He had got two clean hits, one on his neck and one on his chest. When Balwal inquired, the police told him that the young man was called Idrees Bhai. Among other weapons, an M4 carbine was also recovered from the encounter site, which the police assumed had belonged to Kamran. On one rifle magazine, Balwal saw that 'AMMAR' had been written with yellow paint. It was just a gut feeling, but Balwal felt that Idrees Bhai was not an ordinary terrorist – he was someone important. Balwal was told about two phones, an iPhone and a Samsung S-9 Plus, recovered from the two slain terrorists. The police said they were damaged and of no use to them. But Balwal felt that it would be worth a shot for them to be sent for expert examination. On his insistence, the phones were first sent to the Kashmir Police's Cyber Cell. The cell had in October itself acquired a universal forensic extraction device (UFID), used to extract data from mobile phones after bypassing all security measures such as passwords. The experts there tried retrieving the data from the phones but could only open a portion of it. Balwal was convinced that the phones could throw up some vital clues about the Pulwama case.

The problem was that the phones were in the custody of the J&K Police. For further work on this, the NIA investigators felt that a transfer of custody must happen.

In December 2019, the IG Kashmir, S.P. Pani, was transferred. A month later, at a get-together for his farewell, Balwal requested him to help in this matter. He wanted the phones to be sent to the Indian Computer Emergency Response Team (CERT-In), a Central government agency dedicated to ensuring cyber-security. A police officer who was present there recalls that moment. 'Most of us had had a few drinks. Balwal came and told Pani that he was leaving, but it would be of great help if he could give instructions to send that phone to CERT-In,' he said. Luckily, Pani's successor, Vijay Kumar, was also present at the function. Pani called him and pointed at Balwal. 'Please help our friend,' he said. A week later, Balwal's phone rang. It was an expert from CERT-In.

'Sir, we have hit a jackpot,' he said.

~

Just a few days before that call something else had happened that got the NIA team excited about the possibility of some headway in the case. On 31 January 2020, at a toll plaza in Nagrota, on the outskirts of Jammu on the Jammu–Srinagar highway, a truck bearing the number JK03F 1478 was stopped by a police party during a routine check. As they asked for documents, one of the policemen realized that the space between the driver's seat and the cargo hold had a hidden compartment – he was hitting it with a stick and it made a curiously hollow sound. He alerted his colleagues upon which the driver and two other men sitting with him in the front jumped off and ran away, taking advantage of the darkness. At that moment, three Jaish terrorists hiding in the cavity that the policeman had inadvertently discovered opened fire on the police, causing serious injuries to a constable.

While one of the terrorists was killed on the spot in retaliatory fire, the two others initially managed to escape but were later engaged in a nearby forest and killed. The three Kashmiri men in the front seat who had run away turned out to be the handlers of the terrorists. They were later found and arrested. One of them – the driver of the truck – was identified as Sameer Ahmed Dar.

As Sameer Ahmed Dar was interrogated, he revealed that he had been recruited by the Jaish to ferry Pakistani terrorists who had freshly infiltrated into India. Sameer Ahmed Dar's elder brother was also a terrorist with another Pakistan-based organization, the Lashkar-e-Toiba, and had been killed in an encounter with the security forces in the Valley in 2016. The police realized that Sameer Ahmed Dar also happened to be the cousin of the Pulwama suicide bomber, Adil Ahmed Dar!

Sameer told his interrogators that he had been introduced to two Pakistani handlers by a Jaish terrorist, his namesake Sameer Ahmed Dar, known as Hanjila Jihadi.

The Jaish leadership, Sameer confessed, had asked

him to hire other trustworthy people who could help him in his mission of ferrying the three terrorists who had died in the encounter. The Jaish handlers also put him in touch with a Kashmiri student pursuing BSc in Chandigarh, who, in the absence of internet and due to telephone restrictions in Kashmir after the August 2019 abrogation of Article 370, used to act as a messenger between Dar and his Pakistani handlers. He was later arrested from his residence in Budgam in Central Kashmir on 11 February.

On 22 January, Dar and two others he had roped in began their journey to Jodhpur, Rajasthan, carrying a consignment of apples. Once in Punjab, Dar contacted his Pakistani handler on WhatsApp; he was asked to turn back towards Jammu by the end of January as a group would infiltrate then and he would have to take them to the Valley.

After unloading the apples in Jodhpur, the trio loaded pomegranates on to the truck and took them to Amritsar. On 29 January, the handler asked Dar to download a VPN app on his mobile so that he could use the internet anonymously. Mobile internet had been restored in Kashmir four days earlier but usage of WhatsApp was still banned, though it could be used through VPN.

The same night they reached Jammu and stayed inside their truck in the Narwal transport yard, outside Jammu city.

The next day Dar picked up a commercial load of polyvinyl chloride (used often in building and construction) bags from a Jammu locality and created a cavity behind his seat in the truck for the terrorists. Then they went to the market near Jammu's main bus stand in the heart of the city and bought three tracksuits for the terrorists.

On the night of 30–31 January, Dar and his two accomplices reached the pre-decided location: the overhead railway bridge in Samba. At 3 a.m., Dar began to walk towards a dirt track and called out the code given to him: Iqbal. After a few minutes, his call was responded to by one of the terrorists hiding in a bush with his code word: Aijaz.

They had safely made contact. One of the terrorists handed over Rs 50,000 to Dar. Now his task was to hand over the three terrorists to a Jaish commander in Kashmir. The commander had met Dar in December 2019 and asked him to contact him as soon as he crossed the Jawahar Tunnel on the Jammu–Srinagar highway, after which the Valley begins.

Dar was also told that the three terrorists would have with them a packet containing RDX that they should hide somewhere near Samba. But he forgot to do this. By the time he remembered they had already reached Jammu. So, just before the toll plaza where they got exposed, Dar got out and hid the packet in the bushes near a giant billboard on the bypass. To identify the place later, they tied an orange cloth on a pillar nearby and took photos of the spot. The picture was also sent to his handler.

Before this, Dar had successfully managed to place three other terrorists in a safe house in South Kashmir, he told the police.

But this time his luck ran out.

~

Sameer Dar was shown his cousin Adil's video. When he saw it, he told the NIA that the voice in the video was not that of Adil but of Hanjila Jihadi.

The authorities realized that Adil and Hanjila Jihadi had joined the Jaish on the same day in March 2018. 'Both of them often visited a friend who owns a furniture shop,' Sameer Dar said.

That man, the NIA discovered, was none other than

Shakir Bashir – who was in the blue car with Adil on the day of the attack – and his furniture shop was close to the spot where Adil finally struck the CRPF convoy.

As they began looking into details about Bashir, the investigators found out that he had also been picked up by the police as part of their pre-emptive crackdown after the abrogation of Article 370 in August 2019.

They were told that he was to be released on 28 February 2020. As he was being released from a Srinagar courtroom, the NIA team swung into action and took him in their custody. At this point they didn't really know more about his involvement in the Pulwama attack.

This almost coincided with the time when the Samsung S-9 phone recovered from Nowgam was cracked open by CERT-In. It had double encryption that the experts bypassed to recover data worth 100 GB.

As the NIA sought details of the phone from Samsung, they got the address of the Kashmir dealer it was sent to. From the dealer they came to know that it was sold to one Bilal Ahmed Kuchay in August 2018 for Rs 74,000. Though the phone became operational in 2018, it had got synced with the user's cloud storage and had all his data from 2014 onwards.

The first photo Balwal saw in that phone was of a

blue car parked in a house – the house turned out to be that of Shakir Bashir. There was a man in another picture whom he recognized as Shakir Bashir. In another selfie, three men with their faces coated with some sort of silvery powder could be seen. One of them was the bomber, Adil Dar. When he looked closely, Balwal recognized the man taking the selfie as Idrees Bhai. This was the first time that the dots joined to connect Idrees Bhai to Shakir Bashir and Adil Dar, and therefore to the Pulwama attack.

Experts also recovered fifteen to twenty practice versions of Adil's last video. In these videos, there is no flag in the background but a black-coloured wooden almirah with a red border.

Balwal also found a photo of a young woman with Idrees Bhai. She was identified as Insha Jan, the twenty-two-year-old daughter of Peer Tariq Ahmed Shah, a resident of Hakripora, Pulwama. When they were picked up, Insha first told the NIA that she had no idea about which terrorists came to their house as they entered by coercion and they could not do anything to stop them. But when she was confronted with the photo where she is sitting close to Idrees Bhai and holding guns in her hand, she confessed that she and her father were OGWs of the Jaish and that the terrorists had been sent to her house by another Jaish worker and her neighbour.

As their house was searched, Balwal noticed the black-coloured almirah with the red border seen in Adil's video and realized that it had been shot there.

In another photo in Idrees Bhai's phone, the NIA investigators noticed a package from Amazon. They sent the consignment number to the company, which got back saying it was sent to one Waiz-ul-Islam, who had in the last few transactions bought aluminium powder, battery, chargers, knives and a pair of size 13 shoes.

In some videos on the phone, the location tag was that of Sangin camp, a training camp in Afghanistan's Helmand province for the Jaish, Taliban and Al-Qaeda. In some videos, a voice could be heard saying: 'Yeh Sangin camp hai.' This is Sangin camp. In others, Taliban flags were visible. In a few videos, an extremely tall man was seen walking around with some voices in the background asking him to be cautious. 'Ismail Bhai, aage mat jao.' 'Ismail Bhai, udhar mat jao.' Brother Ismail, don't go forward. Brother Ismail, don't go there.

The NIA picked up Bilal Kuchay, the man who bought the phone, and Waiz-ul-Islam, the man in whose name the Amazon orders were placed. Shakir

Bashir was also formally arrested and brought to Jammu for interrogation.

With brownish hair and a scraggy beard, Bashir looked like a university student. As Balwal began interrogating him, he realized that Bashir was a total radical who had no exposure to the world and his only window to the universe was militant Islam. He would repeatedly quote from the Koran the following part of its Surah At-Taubah 9:5 which read:

> Then when the Sacred Months (the first, seventh, eleventh and twelfth months of the Islamic calendar) have passed, then kill the Mushrikun (polytheists) wherever you find them, and capture them and besiege them, and prepare for them each and every ambush.*

Balwal had dealt with many terrorists in the past. But he saw that Bashir was in it because he had total belief that this is what Allah wanted from him. Unlike many others, he was not in this for glamour or for money or for a sense of adventure.

To counter him, Balwal quoted other passages from

---

* Dr M. Muhsin Khan and Dr Taqi-ud-din Hilali, *The Noble Quran*.

the Koran to Bashir, especially the ones that talk about bringing light to the 'non-believer'.

For two days, Balwal played good cop, bad cop with Shakir. Sometimes Balwal would bring food cooked by his wife at home for Bashir. At other times he would threaten him. From his rich experience, Balwal knew that torturing terrorists did not yield results. In many instances, under torture, terrorists would mislead the police to get them off their backs. In Bashir's case, he could see that his approach of evoking memories of food and home was working. The sight of home-cooked food made Bashir emotional. On the third night, he began to cry. *'Ammi ki bohot yaad aa rahi hai'* (I am missing my mother), he said. Balwal made him speak to his mother on the phone. Later, he also gave him books to read.

'He had a puritanical view of Islam. Our officer showed him photos of Idrees Bhai and Insha Jan together. He was in utter disbelief that a man whom he revered could be cosy with women other than his wife,' said a senior official at the NIA headquarters.

One day, as Balwal entered the room Bashir was put in, Bashir looked at him. *'Aapko kuch batana hai'* (I have something to tell you), he said.

'Idrees Bhai is actually Umar Farooq and he is Masood Azhar's nephew and the son of one of the hijackers of the IC-814 plane. He is the one who planned Pulwama.' Indeed, Idrees Bhai or Umar Farooq was none other than the Jaish commander in the Sindhi ajrak topi.

9

The Lover Boy of Bahawalpur

In September of 2016, a young man arrived at a training camp in Afghanistan's Helmand province. The camp was situated in Sangin, a rural district in the province and a major centre of opium trade. It has a unique topography – in some places a desert and in others lush green. In 2009, Sangin was one of the most heavily mined areas in Afghanistan where British troops and the Taliban fought each other for domination.

People in Sangin were mostly landless labourers who worked in the fields during the poppy season and for the rest of the year as mercenaries, fighting for money. Many locals worked both sides, tipping British troops about IEDs and also informing the Taliban about their movement.

The area was so heavily mined that in 2009 the British troops found 1,200 IEDs in just one square kilometre area,* prompting them to call it a 'low-density minefield'. Between April and October 2009, twenty-two British soldiers were killed there.

In 2010, the British troops there were replaced by US Marines. In the first ninety days, around twenty of them were killed in action. The US and UK troops lost more soldiers there than in any of the 400 districts of Afghanistan.

In 2014, the US and British troops left. Three years later, after intense fighting between Afghan forces and the Taliban, Sangin fell completely to the Taliban.

Umar Farooq reached Sangin when the Taliban had gained an upper hand; he stayed in the camp for four months, receiving training on how to make IEDs, in drone technology and in handling machine guns.

His father had arranged this training; Ibrahim Athar Alvi was a liaison person with the Taliban on behalf of the Jaish. Alvi had an old history with India. He was Masood Azhar's brother and also one of the hijackers of the IC-814 plane, which ultimately led to the freedom of Azhar.

In some videos that were found on his phone, Farooq

---

* Jerry Meyerle, Megan Katt and Jim Gavrilis, *On the Ground in Afghanistan: Counterinsurgency in Practice*, Marine Corps University Press, 2012.

is seen trying out an anti-aircraft gun. Around him, his trainers pay compliments gushingly. *'Mashallah, Mashallah,'* one of them says.

In 2017, Umar's training was complete. He returned to Pakistan and began training men in the Jaish camps in Manshera, Balochistan, and the one in Balakot.

In September that year, Masood Azhar first sent one of his nephews, seventeen-year-old Talha Rashid, to fight the Indian forces in Kashmir. He was killed soon afterwards in Pulwama's Aglar Kandi village; an M4 rifle was recovered in Kashmir for the first time, sending the police in a tizzy.

Sometime in January 2018, the Jaish sent Umar Farooq's younger brother, Usman Haider, to Kashmir. He was just seventeen years old, like his cousin Talha Rashid.

The night before, a big party happened in Bahawalpur. This was the norm. Whenever anyone important was to be sent across for jihad, a party would be organized the previous night. When Haider was to be dispatched, the party was attended by, among others, the 'burly man of Bahawalpur', Azhar's brother, Rouf Asgar, the operational head of the Jaish. (Remember, the man in the Sindhi ajrak cap, Umar Farooq, had been exchanging texts with the burly man of Bahawalpur, Rouf Asgar, to get inputs on what to do next and what not to do.) The men danced till midnight and ate heartily. They used an Islamic term for the border crossing – hijrat, which simply means departure, alluding to Prophet Mohammed's migration from Mecca to Medina along with his early followers in 622 CE.

It is not clear why, but just three months later, the Jaish sent Umar Farooq to Kashmir as well. He too infiltrated through the international border in Jammu's Hiranagar sector on the night of 13–14 April 2018.

In the Jaish's rulebook, if an important person is crossing the border, he would come in a group of five. If it were ordinary cadre, they would normally come in a group of three. Umar and four other terrorists sneaked into India through a tunnel. Normally, they would choose a new moon night to infiltrate to escape being spotted.

Umar carried a big M4 carbine rifle and a pistol. The rest carried AK-47s, pistols and grenades. They also brought with them RDX in rucksacks – as much as they could carry comfortably, usually about ten kilos each.

Days before they were to be launched, they would practise with the weapons they were supposed to carry. This training happened in Narowal, in Pakistan's

Punjab province, which shares its border with J&K. Investigation revealed that this is where the Jaish safe houses and launch pads are based.

The group also carried with them what is called a 'matrix sheet'. This one had 1,000 secret codes for communication, for example, how to alert someone in case they spotted BSF troops on the Indian side of the border.

The last hiding place was a spot usually a mere 100 metres away from the border on the Pakistani side. Here, the group would hide in bushes, waiting for an opportune moment to cross. Once they crossed through the tunnel and land on Indian soil, they followed riverine routes to avoid detection. With the help of GPS they would reach a predetermined spot, where a receiving party dispatched from the Valley would be waiting for them.

To receive Umar and his party, a man called Ashiq Ahmed Nengroo and his accomplice, Iqbal Ahmed Rather, had come. Nengroo had once been a police informer. But now he had become a Jaish facilitator, a vital part of its Kashmir operations. The NIA would later find out that between October 2017 and September 2018, Nengroo had made seven trips to Punjab and Jammu and transported thirty-three hardcore Jaish terrorists to the Kashmir Valley, including Umar Farooq and his four accomplices.

Rather, 25, the only brother of seven sisters, had a liberal view of Islam. He came from Chrar, a village in Kashmir's Budgam district, house to the famous Sufi shrine Chrar-e-Sharif. As he was growing up, Rather couldn't help but notice that the crowd of devotees to the shrine had begun to thin out. 'I saw that people were now going to new mosques which had come up all around us,' he would tell the NIA after his arrest. He had just joined a BTech course when he came in touch with Nengroo.

In a few weeks' time, he had quit engineering and joined a nursing course. Nengroo had radicalized him and told him that the nursing course would come in handy while treating injured mujahids.

After picking up Umar and party, Nengroo began his journey towards Jammu, and then onwards to the Kashmir Valley, in his truck with the registration number JK03G 1621. Rather drove ahead in his Fiat Punto, JK01Q 4551, so as to alert Nengroo of any security presence on the road.

From the international border onwards, Umar sat with Nengroo in the front keeping only a pistol with him. The rest of the terrorists were hidden in a cavity behind the driver's seat along with other weapons.

By morning they were at the transport yard in Narwal, on the outskirts of Jammu city, where they realized that the Jammu–Srinagar highway was closed for some reason. They waited at a dhaba there. Rather drove a little ahead and got biryani for them from a Muslim-run restaurant.

At night, they resumed their journey towards Srinagar. They reached the Kashmir Valley early in the morning on 15 April and were provided shelter at Nengroo's house.

Later, Umar was introduced to Bilal Ahmed Kuchay, 28, a rich Kashmiri, who owned a sawmill. Kuchay was also a sympathizer, and soon, from Nengroo's house, Umar shifted to his house. It is here that Hanjila Jihadi brought Adil Ahmed Dar who he said was ready to work with the Jaish.

At Kuchay's house, Umar noticed a young man whom Kuchay had deputed to bring food for them every afternoon.

'Who is he?' he asked Kuchay.

Kuchay told him that his name was Shakir Bashir. 'He is not Deobandi but Ahle-Hadith,' he said. The Jaish adheres to the Deobandi school that advocates Islamic conservatism, but Ahle-Hadith is also puritanical, often compared with Saudi Arabia's Wahhabism.

'It doesn't matter; we are all destined to follow Allah's path,' Farooq replied.

Umar began getting close to Shakir, who was deeply influenced by Umar. Taking him into confidence later, Umar told him that he suspected Kuchay was also helping the police with a little information here and there.

But it was Kuchay who got a Samsung S-9 mobile phone for Umar from Gulshan Electronics in Budgam.

Sometime later in 2018, a man called Ismail also crossed the international border and reached Kashmir. He was extremely tall, which earned him the code name Lamboo (the tall one). It was he who was seen in some videos recovered from Umar Farooq's phone where he was being asked to be careful. One of his other code names was Saifullah (sword of Islam). This, the NIA believed, was given only to very important terrorist commanders. There were indications that he was also from Masood Azhar's family.

While Umar Farooq was working on Adil and Shakir and others, Lamboo worked on a young student, Waiz-ul-Islam, a resident of the posh Bagh-e-Mehtab area in Srinagar. He was excellent at studies and wanted to become a doctor. Lamboo worked slowly on him, poisoning his mind. In private conversations, they made fun of him, calling him Waiz bhola (simpleton). His Amazon account was used to buy cargo pants, knives, mobile covers, laser pointers. Through Waiz's account, Lamboo also bought camping shoes in size 13 for his big feet. Waiz drove a gearless scooter and delivered all these items regularly to the Jaish men on a bypass road.

On 30 October 2018, Umar Farooq's brother, Usman Haider, was killed in an encounter with the security forces in Tral. After his death, Masood Azhar released an audio statement from Pakistan. He told Kashmiris that their blood should boil at a seventeen-year-old boy's 'martyrdom' and that Kashmiri youth should follow his path.

It was after Usman's death that the Jaish decide to seek revenge by carrying out a big attack.

At Bilal Kuchay's house, Umar Farooq made Adil Dar hear Azhar's audio. Dar was so moved that he told Farooq he was ready to follow the 'Sheikh's (Azhar's) directions' and attain 'shahadat' (martyrdom).

Sajjad Bhat meanwhile was sent to select a car. He checked out a few, but ultimately found a Maruti Eeco for sale. The car, he realized, suited their task well –

its middle seat was already removed and the car was still registered in the name of its first owner. The car was procured in the last week of January. Shakir Bashir drove it to his home and parked it in the front yard. He worked diligently with an iron filer, erasing the engine and chassis numbers.

In January, Waiz was asked to buy three kilos of aluminium powder, which he did through his Amazon account.

Mudasir Khan procured gelatine sticks, easily available in Kashmir since it was used for road construction and in cement factories.

Shakir Bashir purchased a few bags of ammonium nitrate from a fertilizer shop in Pulwama. He also purchased a blue-coloured mixing drum and an orange-coloured can.

Around the same time, Umar shifted to Insha Jan's house. (He had stayed there briefly on two previous occasions.) The family had been introduced to him by their neighbour, Abbas Rather. Rather was a police informer, but also worked for the Jaish and Lashkar as a mercenary. Insha Jan's father, Peer Tariq Shah, was also sympathetic to terrorists; one of his cousins and a nephew were both terrorists who got killed in encounters with security forces.

Insha, 22, was attracted to Umar. She began to spend time with him and Umar also gave her a lot of attention. He was married to one Afeera Bibi, who was in Pakistan. But in Kashmir, Insha became his lover, his temporary wife, taking care of his needs. Umar provided her with a Redmi Note 5 Pro mobile phone so that he could stay in touch with her through WhatsApp voice calls. Umar changed his number frequently, she told NIA investigators, and also advised her to change her number often. But she was unable to do this.

On her request, Umar took her pictures with his guns. Umar and his friends would come to her house every ten to fifteen days and stay for a few days. She told the police that they mostly stayed inside the house and at night took turns to keep a watch around the house from inside the attic.

As they became more intimate, Umar also introduced Insha to his mother and sister in Pakistan on WhatsApp video calls. Once, he even made her speak to his wife. Terrorists fighting in Kashmir often have lovers among Kashmiri women.

In the first week of February 2019, Umar and Adil and Hanjila came to stay at Insha's house with heavy weapons. This time, Insha told investigators, Adil stayed silent, spending most of his time in prayer.

Here, in Insha Jan's home, Adil Ahmed Dar's final video was rehearsed several times against the backdrop of the black-coloured cupboard with the red border. Dar kept faltering in his speech, so Hanjila Jihadi was made to dub the video. When they were satisfied, the video was sent to Pakistan to Ammar Alvi, another brother of Masood Azhar and an uncle of Umar Farooq. It was his name 'AMMAR' that Balwal had seen painted on one of the magazines found by Umar's dead body.

The final edited video was sent back to them from Pakistan on 4 February 2019. The same day, on Umar Farooq's instructions, Shakir Bashir bought two Exide batteries and digital multimeters (used for the testing of electric detonators and blasting circuits) from Srinagar.

On the evening of 5 February, Umar, Adil Ahmed Dar, Hanjila Jihadi and Shakir Bashir drove in Bashir's car to his house. It is a day that Pakistan observes as Kashmir Day.

Umar, an explosives expert, put RDX and ammonium nitrate and gelatine sticks in three layers and then wired the explosive device. He also used the aluminium powder bought by Waiz-ul-Islam as 'binder' – Umar told them that with this the target would catch fire easily. It was this powder that was smeared on their faces when Umar took a selfie with Adil and Hanjila.

The Maruti Eeco car was already in place. In all, they put 160 kg of explosives in the blue drum and 40 kg in the orange can and joined the wires to a switch beneath the steering wheel. Throughout this exercise, Umar was in touch with his uncles, seeking directions. The plan was to attack a convoy on 6 February.

But on the night of 5 February it snowed heavily. The Jammu–Kashmir national highway was closed, resulting in a halt on convoy movement.

Umar, Adil and Hanjila stayed put at Shakir's house. The car with 200 kg of explosives remained parked in his front yard.

On the afternoon of 14 February, Shakir Bashir was in his furniture shop when he noticed the CRPF's ROP being deployed on the highway. He immediately informed Umar Farooq that the convoy movement would begin shortly. At 2 p.m., Umar left the house to do a recce himself. Once he was back, he told Shakir and Adil to leave immediately. Adil took a pistol along in case the IED did not detonate.

At the spot, Adil's hands were trembling. Shakir told NIA investigators that Adil was very scared of Umar. He said that from the day he was chosen as the suicide bomber Umar did not allow him to have any contact with anyone.

When Shakir returned after dropping off Adil, he found that Hanjila Jihadi and Umar had left his house and shifted back to Insha Jan's house. After some time Shakir returned to the spot of the attack and clicked pictures of the blood and gore. The plan was to release them later to dampen the morale of security forces operating in Kashmir. But after Balakot, this idea was dropped.

After returning he told Umar and the others that he had heard senior CRPF officials at the site utter a figure of forty dead. This they conveyed to their handlers in Pakistan. This figure was then published by *Al-Qalam* in its new edition – before the CRPF had made it public.

By this time, Insha had seen Adil's video on TV. She realized that the video was shot in her house. She asked Hanjila why Adil chose to go like this when he couldn't even meet his parents one last time. Hanjila replied that Adil himself had chosen this way.

Insha noticed that after the attack both Umar and Hanjila were very happy. Umar and Hanjila stayed at Insha Jan's place for three days. Umar asked Insha's father to construct one more room on the first floor which they could use regularly for hiding. He said he would pay for the construction.

Shakir was also ready to become a suicide bomber. Umar told him that he should be prepared for a mission. In March 2019, Shakir told NIA investigators that he had conducted more recces for other attacks. The site for an attack and explosives for it were also put in place. This time Umar wanted him to be the bomber. But he told Umar that first he wanted to be active as a fighter in the field, after which he would be willing to die for Allah. He was given the code name of Abu Huzaifah. So they decided that they would use some other boy from Tral instead. But this attack was later put on hold by the burly man of Bahawalpur, Rouf Asgar.

In the middle of March, Umar and Hanjila returned to Insha's house and stayed for a few days.

After the Pulwama attack, Rouf Asgar asked his nephew to delete the chat history on his mobile phone and to destroy the phone. But Umar didn't do this. Instead, he destroyed another cheap phone and sent a picture of the destroyed decoy phone as evidence to Asgar.

On 29 March, when he was shot in the encounter in his Nowgam hideout, Umar tried to destroy the phone. But it was only partially damaged.

It was this phone that Balwal laid his hands upon. Without the mobile phone Umar left behind, it would have been very difficult to establish the Pulwama attack conspiracy all the way to Masood Azhar and his brothers.

It was just one small mistake Umar committed that led to their encounter. But what was that mistake? The investigators requested for that not to be made public. Had Umar not made that one mistake Kamran and he would have gone unnoticed, planning other attacks on security forces. The security agencies wouldn't have even known of their existence.

Ten days after Umar's death, Hanjila visited Insha and told her about his death. She told NIA investigators that at first she did not believe him. But Hanjila showed her the pictures of his corpse. He then asked her to hand over to him the Redmi phone that Umar had gifted her. As Insha looked on, Hanjila took out the SIM and broke it. Then he took away the phone. After that, he never returned.

As Insha grieved for Umar, she was oblivious to some facts. The data extraction from Umar's phone also threw up his intimate communication with other women. Investigation revealed that Umar also took shelter at the house of Insha's paternal aunt. During his stay there he became intimate with Insha's cousin sister. The voice messages between the two in which their intimacy was established were also recovered from Umar's phone.

The investigation also revealed that just before Adil Dar became a suicide bomber, he had sent a will of sorts to his father, indicating that he would not be around for much longer. But senior Dar kept this to himself, and waited for the news of his son's death to arrive.

Shakir Bashir revealed the entire blueprint of the attack in front of a magistrate.

In March 2020, the NIA took Shakir Bashir to his home in Pulwama, along with a magistrate, to establish evidence in the case. His mother fainted at the sight of her son. Outside, a hostile crowd began to swell. It took the NIA team some effort to extricate themselves safely.

As Waiz's involvement was established, his mother would not stop crying. She told the NIA investigators that her son had been born after a lot of prayers and she had no idea how he got influenced by radicals. Inside the courtroom, Waiz kept crying, later saying he had made a huge mistake.

Last heard, in a jail in Jammu, he was made the in-charge of the library; he asked for books to prepare for medical entrance exams, which were provided to him.

The case – *State versus Masood Azhar and (16) others* – is now in a Jammu court.

~

After Umar Farooq's death, the Jaish appointed Qari Yasir as its Kashmir chief. In January 2020, Yasir was killed in an encounter with the security forces. After Yasir, a man called Mohammed Idrees alias Fauji (from Multan in Pakistan) was appointed as the chief. He too was killed in an encounter in June. Fauji, suspected to be a relative of Masood Azhar, had planned another attack like Pulwama, but it was averted just in time by the security forces a few days before he was gunned down.

At present, the Jaish chief in Kashmir is a man called Abdullah Rashid Ghazi, who, according to the police, is operating from Tral. In the Jaish hierarchy in Kashmir, he is succeeded by Lamboo, who is also believed to be a relative of Azhar. The police believe he operates from Pulwama only and managed to escape twice from security cordons. After them comes Hanjila Jihadi.

~

In February 2021, a joint team of police from J&K arrested a terrorist, Hidayatullah Malik, from the outskirts of Jammu city. Malik is from Shopian and was heading an organization called Lashkar-e-Mustafa, which the police believe is a front of the Jaish. Sometime earlier, Malik had taken a flight to Delhi to conduct a recce of the office of the National Security Adviser Ajit Doval. He had made a video of the location and sent it to his handler in Pakistan.

Malik's interrogation revealed that he had escorted Ashiq Ahmed Nengroo, the man who helped Umar enter Kashmir from the LoC, and his wife and children from Kashmir to a tunnel in Samba on the international border in December 2018. From there, Nengroo and his family fled to Pakistan. Malik told the interrogators that twenty minutes after entering the tunnel in Samba, he received a call from Nengroo. He told Malik that he had reached safely and was now having tea with his Pakistani handlers. Nengroo is believed to be in a Jaish camp now.

Nengroo's associate Iqbal Rather was arrested in July 2020.

The tunnel in Samba's Galar village that Nengroo used to escape was detected by the BSF in August 2020. Like other tunnels, this one was enforced with sandbags carrying markings of Karachi and Shakargarh, the area just across the border in Pakistan's Narowal district.

But sources from the Kashmir Police say there could be many undetected tunnels in the sector that Pakistan will continue to use to carry out terrorist activities in Kashmir and elsewhere in India.

The terrorist network based in Pakistan is now also using drones to send weapons to India. These weapons, just like men, are picked up by Kashmiri OGWs from the border. In the eventuality of heightened security along the international border, police sources reveal that the Jaish may shift to using the Nepal route to send its terrorists.

'The relay race continues,' said a senior police officer in Kashmir. 'They come, we kill.'

But in between their coming and getting killed, sometimes attacks like Pulwama happen.

'We will have to kill the dragon head sitting in Bahawalpur,' said a police officer in Kashmir, referring to Masood Azhar.

But till that happens, he and his brothers will always aim for India's jugular.

The Jaish Poison Ivy

Masood Azhar Alvi, 52. Founder of terrorist organization Jaish-e-Mohammed. At large in Pakistan.

Rouf Asgar Alvi, 47. Younger brother of Masood Azhar, operational head of the Jaish. Was in charge of the operation that led to the Pulwama suicide attack. At large in Pakistan.

Ammar Alvi, 45. Youngest brother of Masood Azhar. Was in charge of slipping Jaish terrorists, including his nephew, Umar Farooq, into Kashmir. At large in Pakistan.

Umar Farooq, 24. Nephew of Masood Azhar. The Jaish commander responsible for planning the Pulwama suicide attack. Killed in Kashmir.

Adil Ahmed Dar, 21. The Jaish terrorist who carried out the suicide attack in February 2019.

Shakir Bashir, 24. Kashmiri Jaish OGW who sheltered Jaish terrorists in his house, carried out reconnaissance for the attack and later drove Dar to the spot of the attack. Under arrest now.

Sameer Ahmed Dar, alias Hanjila Jihadi, 22. Jaish terrorist. Helped put explosives together. Currently number three in the Jaish hierarchy in Kashmir.

Insha Jan, 22. Pulwama resident, lover of Umar Farooq. Provided shelter to Umar Farooq and others. Under arrest now.

Waiz-ul-Islam, 19. Jaish OGW. Used his Amazon account to buy, among other things, aluminium powder (used in bomb-making) for the terrorists. Under arrest now.

Mohammed Ismail alias Lamboo, 25. Jaish commander, believed to be a relative of Masood Azhar. Part of the conspiracy. Now the most wanted Jaish commander in Kashmir.

Bilal Kuchay, 28. Jaish OGW. Introduced Shakir Bashir to Umar Farooq, bought mobile phones for the terrorists. Under arrest now.

Ashiq Ahmed Nengroo, 33. Jaish OGW. Responsible for ferrying Umar Farooq and several other Jaish terrorists to Kashmir from the international border in Jammu. Fled to Pakistan.

Sajjad Ahmed Bhat, 19. The Jaish terrorist who arranged the car used in the suicide attack. Killed in an encounter.

Mudasir Khan, 24. Jaish terrorist. Procured gelatine sticks for the bomb. Killed in an encounter.

Noor Mohammed Tantray, 47. Jaish terrorist. Mastermind of several big attacks on security forces in Kashmir. Helped create the Jaish network in Kashmir. Killed in 2017.

Ghazi Baba, mid-30s. Jaish's first chief in Kashmir, mastermind of the 2001 Parliament attack. Killed in 2003.

Author's Note

This book is based on my own reporting and on evidence provided by primary sources, unless stated otherwise. For the case of the Pulwama suicide attack, I have relied upon officers of the NIA and J&K Police, who were directly involved in the investigation. At every stage, the events described in the book were corroborated at multiple levels with other agencies involved in counter-insurgency operations in and outside Kashmir. These include sources in the Indian Army, CRPF, BSF, Delhi Police's Special Cell and RAW. They are unnamed because of obvious reasons.

I have also spoken to various other individuals in Kashmir, in places like Tral and downtown Srinagar, who have been privy to some of the incidents I have included in the book. For the Ghazi Baba story, the BSF officer Narendra Nath Dhar Dubey has come on record for the first time. Again, at every stage, the trajectory of this story has been verified with multiple other sources, including officers of the J&K Police and the army's military intelligence.

I have personally visited all the flashpoints mentioned in the book, such as the spot where the attack took place, Hajibal and Tral in Pulwama, Shopian, popular infiltration routes along the LoC in North Kashmir and the international border in Samba, Jammu, where the tunnels used by the Jaish commanders to sneak into Kashmir were discovered.

I also met former militants who were active in the 1990s and early 2000s, and several people who knew the Jaish terrorists and OGWs mentioned in the book.

I also made attempts to meet Insha Jan, Shakir Bashir and others in jail for an interview, but permission for the same was denied by the authorities.

CRAFTED FOR MOBILE READING

Thought you would never read a book on mobile? Let us prove you wrong.

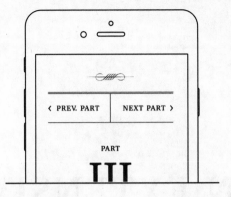

Beautiful Typography

The quality of print transferred
to your mobile. Forget ugly PDFs.

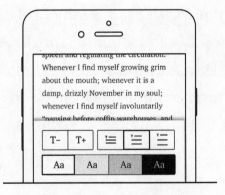

Customizable Reading

Read in the font size, spacing
and background of your liking.

AN EXTENSIVE LIBRARY

Including fresh, new, original Juggernaut books from the likes of Sunny Leone, Praveen Swami, Husain Haqqani, Umera Ahmed, Rujuta Diwekar and lots more. Plus, books from partner publishers and loads of free classics. Whichever genre you like, there's a book waiting for you.

DON'T JUST READ; INTERACT

We're changing the reading experience from passive to active.

Ask authors questions

Get all your answers from the horse's mouth.
Juggernaut authors actually reply to every
question they can.

Rate and review

Let everyone know of your favourite reads or
critique the finer points of a book – you will be
heard in a community of like-minded readers.

Gift books to friends

For a book-lover, there's no nicer gift than
a book personally picked. You can even
do it anonymously if you like.

Enjoy new book formats

Discover serials released in parts over
time, picture books including comics,
and story-bundles at discounted rates.
And coming soon, audiobooks.

4

LOWEST PRICES & ONE-TAP BUYING

Books start at ₹10 with regular discounts and free previews.

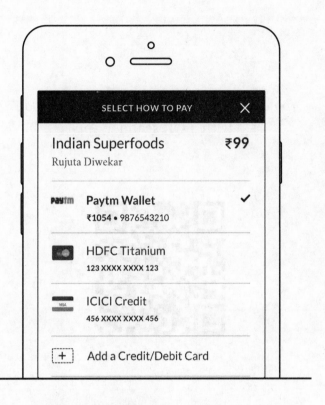

Paytm Wallet, Cards & Apple Payments

On Android, just add a Paytm Wallet once and buy any book with one tap. On iOS, pay with one tap with your iTunes-linked debit/credit card.

To download the app scan the QR Code
with a QR scanner app

For our complete catalogue, visit www.juggernaut.in
To submit your book, send a synopsis and two
sample chapters to books@juggernaut.in
For all other queries, write to contact@juggernaut.in